THE
Context
OF *Holiness*

THE
Context
OF *Holiness*

Psychological and Spiritual Reflections
on the Life of St. Thérèse of Lisieux

Revised Edition

Marc Foley, O.C.D.

ICS Publications
Institute of Carmelite Studies
Washington, D.C.

ICS Publications
2131 Lincoln Road NE
Washington, DC 20002-1199
www.icspublications.org

© Washington Province of Discalced Carmelites Inc., 2008.
Revised Edition 2020 by ICS Publications.

All rights reserved. No part of this book may be reproduced or transmitted in any form or by any means, electronic or mechanical, including photocopying, recording, or by any information, storage or retrieval system without prior written permission from the publisher.

Cover and text design and pagination by Rose Design
Printed in the United States of America

ISBN: 978-1-939272-88-1 (Revised Edition pbk)
ISBN: 978-1-939272-87-4 (ebook)

The Library of Congress has cataloged the first edition as follows:
Foley, Marc, 1949
   The context of holiness : psychological and spiritual reflections on the life of St. Thérèse of Lisieux / by Marc Foley.
      159 p. ; 22 cm.
   Includes bibliographical references (p. 145-159).
   ISBN 978 0 935216 46 2
1.   Thérèse, de Lisieux, Saint, 1873 1897. I. Title.
BX4700.T5F65 2008
282.092 dc22
                2008026517

To Kirstie Green

In Appreciation:

To my dear friend Sandra Gettings, for the many hours she spent helping me write this book.

Contents

Abbreviations	ix
The Context of Holiness	1
The Wounds of Childhood	5
A Nurturing and Healing Atmosphere	15
The Halcyon Days of Youth	24
The Distressing Years	37
The Gathering Storm	53
But You Promised	61
Pauline Is Lost to Me	67
A Sorrow Too Deep for Tears	73
A Gradual Awakening	86
The Battle of Bearing Her Emotions	95
The Martyrdom of Scruples	100
The Uncertain Certainty	122
The Undramatic Drama	144
Notes	149

Abbreviations

St. Thérèse of Lisieux

All quotations of St. Thérèse are taken from the John Clarke, O.C.D., translations of her works published by ICS Publications
The abbreviations used in this book are as follows:

    S   *Story of a Soul*
    LC *The Last Conversations*
    L   *The Collected Letters*
    PT *The Poetry of St. Thérèse*

The number following the letter refers to the page of the ICS edition of the work cited. Thus, (S 13) refers to page thirteen of *Story of a Soul*, 3rd ed. (Washington, D.C.: ICS Publications, 1996).

St. John of the Cross

All quotations of St. John of the Cross are taken from *The Collected Works of St. John of the Cross*, trans. Kieran Kavanaugh, O.C.D., and Otilio Rodriguez, O.C.D. (Washington, D.C.: ICS Publications, 1991).
The abbreviations of John's works are as follows:

    A   *The Ascent of Mount Carmel*
    N   *The Dark Night of the Soul*
    C   *The Spiritual Canticle*
    F   *The Living Flame of Love*
    Co *The Counsels*

Regarding references to both *The Ascent of Mount Carmel* and *The Dark Night of the Soul*, the first number indicates the book, the second number refers to the chapter, and the third number refers to the paragraph. For example, (A 2.3.4) refers to book two, chapter three, paragraph four of The Ascent. In like manner, for *The Spiritual Canticle* and *The Living Flame of Love*, the first number refers to the stanza and the second number to the paragraph. Thus, (C 3.4) is a reference to stanza three, paragraph four of *The Spiritual Canticle*.

St. Teresa of Ávila

All quotes from St. Teresa of Ávila's *The Way of Perfection* are taken from *The Collected Works of Saint Teresa of Avila,* vol. 2, trans. Kieran Kavanaugh, O.C.D., and Otilio Rodriguez, O.C.D. (Washington, D.C.: ICS Publications, 1980).

The abbreviations of John's works are as follows:

W   *The Way of Perfection*

Regarding references, the first number refers to the chapter and the second number to the paragraph. Thus, (W 4.6) refers to chapter four, paragraph six.

The Context of Holiness

To say that this book is about the spiritual life of St. Thérèse of Lisieux is to make a nebulous statement at best. The phrase *the spiritual life*, writes Evelyn Underhill, "is a dangerously ambiguous term," which has fallen prey to many misconceptions and aberrations, as the history of spirituality clearly demonstrates.[1] One such misconception is that the spiritual life is an encapsulated sphere, cloistered from the realities of daily living.

The basic premise of this book is that we have only *one life* composed of *various dimensions*. Our emotional life, intellectual life, social life, work life, sex life, spiritual life are simply ways of speaking of the *different* facets of our *one* life.

The spiritual life is our journey home to God, by which we wend our way along serpentine paths through the dark forest of our multidimensional existence, with neither a detailed roadmap to guide us nor adequate light to read the road signs clearly. This is not a definition of the spiritual life but rather a description with which we can all identify. Abbé de Tourville, a French spiritual writer who lived in Tourville, France during the years when Thérèse's family spent their holidays there, wrote the following:

> I wish so much that you could get hold of the idea of what perfection in this world consists of. It is not like going up a great hill from which we see an ever-widening landscape, a greater horizon, a plain receding further and further into the distance. It is more like an overgrown path, which we cannot find; we grope about; we are caught by brambles; we lose all sense of distance covered; we do not know whether we are going round

and round or whether we are advancing. We are certain only of one thing, that we desire to go on even though we are worn out and tired. That is your life and you should rejoice greatly because of it, for it is a true life, serious and real, on which God opens His eyes and His heart.[2]

Thérèse's life was a real life. As it unfolds before us on the pages of *Story of a Soul*, we see a pilgrim soul who made its way home to God through many raging storms and dark nights. The specific nature of Thérèse's trials may differ from our own, but their psychological and emotional sufferings we all share. For example, we may not have known the pain of our mother dying when we were four, but we all have known the pain of the loss of a loved one. The sufferings that we share with Thérèse are universal—physical pain, anxiety, anger, sadness, depression, loneliness, doubts of faith, to name a few. These sufferings make doing the will of God difficult, but they are the context of our choices. They are the context of holiness.

In the following pages, we will explore many of Thérèse's choices to do the will of God within their physical, psychological, and emotional contexts. It is my hope that such an investigation will not only give us insight into the heroic nature of Thérèse's choices but will also give us encouragement as we face similar choices on our journey home to God.

The Use of Psychology. Before we begin our consideration, it is important that I say a few words about the use of modern psychology in this book. In our day, psychology has often been misused to reduce the spiritual to the psychological. Such abuses, however, should not blind us to the help that modern science can provide in the investigation of matters of faith. Both faith and reason are lights given by God. "Since the same God who reveals mysteries and infuses faith has bestowed the light of reason on the human mind . . . consequently, methodical research in all branches of knowledge, provided it is carried out in a truly scientific manner and does not override moral laws, can never conflict with the faith, because the things of the world and the things of faith derive from the same God" (Catechism of the Catholic Church 159).

Just as medieval theologians, such as St. Augustine and St. Thomas Aquinas, used the thought of pagan philosophers to help explain the truths of faith, so too the Church in our time recognizes the useful role of the social sciences in this regard. "In pastoral care sufficient use should be made, not only of theological principles, but also of the findings of secular sciences, especially psychology and sociology: in this way the faithful will be brought to a purer and more mature living of the faith" (The Pastoral Constitution on the Church in the Modern World 62).

Psychology can be a helpful *tool* in understanding the dynamics of human growth and the spiritual life, provided we do not make it a *touchstone*. To do so is to risk falling prey to what St. Thomas Aquinas considered the weakest of all arguments, the argument from authority: "the argument from authority based on human reason is the weakest" (*Summa Theologiae* [ST] I, q. 1, a. 8, ad 2). Thomas never quoted Aristotle just because Aristotle *said* it, but because he believed what Aristotle said was *true*. Even though Thomas relied heavily upon Aristotle's philosophy as a vehicle to expound the truths of the Christian faith, he did not blind himself to the fact that Aristotle held many views that were contrary to Christian belief. "[St. Thomas] never assumed that the doctrine of Aristotle was invariably compatible with Christian doctrine. This attitude was quite prevalent among medieval Aristotelians. Thomas himself was never one of this number; we find him speaking of those who vainly endeavor to prove that Aristotle said nothing against the faith."[3]

In short, we should never swallow a school of thought whole; we should sift the wheat from the chaff, separate truth from falsehood. As St. Thomas wrote of St. Augustine's use of Platonic philosophy: "whenever Augustine, who was imbued with the doctrines of the Platonists, found in their teaching anything consistent with faith, he adopted it: and those things which he found contrary to faith he amended" (ST I, q. 84, a. 5).

We should never reject a system of thought outright simply because *some* of its tenants may be false. We need to ask what part is *true*; what ideas, concepts, paradigms, models of thought, etc., can be *useful* in elucidating matters of faith. As St. John of the Cross put it, regarding his treatment of the spiritual life: "I will not *rely* on experience or science . . . [but] I will not *neglect* whatever possible use I can make of them" (A Prol 2, emphases added).[4] In short, we should not fail to employ a tool simply because it has limited value. A case in point is my use of the psychology of Sigmund Freud in trying to understand the mysterious illness Thérèse suffered when she was ten years old. Why Freud? Why would I subject the Little Flower to the psychological scalpel of this "completely Godless Jew," as Freud once referred to himself? Why would I employ the psychological system of a man who believed that religion was an illusion? I employ it for a very simply reason. While I do not accept Freud's philosophical and theological beliefs, I have found that his explanation of the role of repression in neurotic episodes is the most helpful one for shedding light on Thérèse's illness. This is an example of separating the wheat from the chaff. In this book, I employed the insights derived from different schools of psychology. My criterion for which school I used at any particular time was its *usefulness* in elucidating an aspect of Thérèse's life. I pray that this book will deepen your appreciation of St. Thérèse's holiness as it enriches your understanding of the context of her life.

The Wounds of Childhood

THERE ARE CERTAIN EVENTS IN life—deaths, births, marriages, divorces, and critical life choices—that cut life in two. They determine "before" and "after" for us. They are definitive moments after which life will never be the same. The death of St. Thérèse's mother was such an event for her; it differentiated the periods of her life. "The first [period] . . . extends from the dawn of my reason till our dear mother's departure for heaven. . . . [The second period] . . . extends from the age of four and a half [when Thérèse's mother died] to that of fourteen, the time when I found once again my *childhood* character, and entered more and more into the serious side of life" (S 16, 34). In short, the death of Thérèse's mother was so traumatic that it determined how she experienced the different chapters of her life; it became her inner reference point. Thérèse experienced herself as she was *before* her mother died; how she was *after* her mother died; and how she was when she regained what she had lost *at the time* of her mother's death.

The death of Thérèse's mother changed her personality and how she related to the world. "My happy disposition completely changed after Mama's death. I, once so full of life, became timid and retiring, sensitive to an excessive degree. One look was enough to reduce me to tears, and the only way I was content was to be left alone completely. I could not bear the company of strangers and found my joy only within the intimacy of the family" (S 34–35).

To explain this drastic change, we need to explore two interrelated realities. First, Thérèse's history of early childhood separation experiences from mother figures *before* her mother's death. Second, the emotional state of Thérèse's mother Zélie in the years both prior to and after Thérèse's birth. Together, they will help us understand Thérèse's vulnerability *at the time* of Zélie's death.

Early Separation Experiences. At three months of age, Thérèse was separated from her mother. Because of Thérèse's poor health and her refusal to nurse, she was brought to Rose Taille, a wet nurse, who lived on a farm in Semallé, several miles from Alençon. Thérèse lived with Rose for eleven months.[5]

During this first critical year of life, when the foundations of personality are laid, Thérèse bonded with Rose "as mother." This is indicated by the fact that Rose became the place of refuge for Thérèse in times of anxiety. For example, on market days, when Rose came to Alençon and brought Thérèse to the Martin household, Thérèse would cling to Rose as a frightened child would cling to her mother. Guy Gaucher writes: "Thérèse became a real country girl . . . and she found it hard to readjust to town life. If, during one of her frequent visits home, one of her mother's smart customers picked her up she would scream, terrified by their hairstyles and above all their hats. She did not want to leave Rose, and to avoid screams and tantrums they had to let her go and sit at the market stall with her nurse."[6]

Zélie was not the mothering presence in Thérèse's life during this time. Rose was. This is illustrated in the following event. One day when Rose brought Thérèse to the Martin household, there were several of Zélie's employees present, all peasant women like Rose. Zélie writes, "Working women are coming to me each moment, and I was giving her [Thérèse] to one and then another. She really wanted to see them, *even more willingly than to see me,* and she kissed them several times. Country women dressed like the wet nurse, this is the world she needs!" (L 1208, emphasis added). Such events indicate that Thérèse bonded with anyone who resembled Rose and was frightened by anyone who did not.

At fifteen months, Thérèse was taken away from Rose and brought back home. Thus, Thérèse suffered two separations from mother figures during the first critical year of life. A common effect of such separations is that they engender in a child a pervasive apprehensiveness that she will be abandoned again.[7] There are indications that this was true for Thérèse.

Zélie wrote the following to her daughter Pauline on June 25, 1874, when Thérèse was eighteen months old: "The little one has just placed her hand on my face and kissed me. This poor little thing doesn't want to leave me; she's continually at my side. She likes going into the garden, but when I'm not there she won't stay but cries till they bring her to me" (S 18). Such clinging behavior is not abnormal in a child of eighteen months. Nevertheless, we need to consider Zélie's concern in the light of the fact that she is an experienced mother who had already raised several children. It is as if Zélie is saying to Pauline, "There is something wrong with her; Thérèse's fear is excessive." Also, Zélie describes Thérèse as a "nervous child" (S 23).[8] This comment is very significant because it refers to an aspect of Thérèse's personality that underlies her clinging behavior. Let us try to understand this behavior within the psychological framework of Margaret Mahler.

According to Mahler, the first few months of an infant's existence is lived within a single psychic universe with its mother. The infant has either no awareness or a rudimentary awareness of itself as a distinct being from its mother. Toward the end of the second month or the beginning of the third month (when Thérèse suffered her first separation), the infant "hatches" psychologically. That is, it has developed an awareness of itself as a distinct entity from its mother. In consequence, the infant is vulnerable to separation anxiety. If the infant could verbalize its feelings it might say the following: "If I am *distinct* from mother, then I can be *separated from* her."

Around the ninth month, the infant enters what Mahler calls the "practicing" phase of separation, which consists of the infant "practicing" leaving mother. It crawls away from mother in order to explore the wonderful world around it but quickly returns for "emotional refueling." Mother is becoming less and less someone to *cling to* and more of a safe home base to *return to*. The infant is dealing with a conflict that all of us struggle with in daily life. We might call this struggle the tension between security and adventure, intimacy and autonomy, or closeness and distance. None of us want to be either abandoned or trapped by people; we don't want to be either locked into or locked out of a relationship. We say to people, "Don't leave me, but give me my space." We all try to protect ourselves from both *separation anxiety* and *suffocation anxiety*. And depending upon early childhood experiences, among other factors, each of us is more vulnerable to one of these two anxieties. Thérèse had a considerable amount of separation anxiety that was engendered by early separations from mother figures.

The words of Zélie that we quoted above indicate this reality. "The little one has just placed her hand on my face and kissed me. This poor little thing *doesn't want to leave me*; *she's continually at my side*. She likes going into the garden, but when I'm not there she won't stay but cries till they bring her to me" (S 18, emphasis added). Zélie wrote these words when Thérèse was several months beyond the *end* of Mahler's practicing phase of separation. This indicates that Thérèse exhibited a high degree of separation anxiety for her age. This should not surprise us considering Thérèse's early separations from Zélie and

Rose. But there was another factor that contributed to Thérèse being a "nervous child"; it was Zélie's anxiety.

Zélie's Emotional State before and after Thérèse's Birth. Zélie did not have a happy childhood. In a letter to her brother Isidore Guérin, she wrote: "My childhood and youth were as dismal as a winding sheet [a shroud]; although my mother spoiled you, she was very severe with me as you know. Even though she was very good, she did not know how to take me, and I suffered very much interiorly" (S 2). This lack of maternal bonding may have been one of the root causes of a "restless and often melancholic temperament" (S 2) that is evident in Zélie's letters. Besides her melancholic temperament, there were several other factors that contributed to making Zélie anxious and depressed both prior to and after Thérèse's birth.

First, there were the daily cares, worries, and preoccupations that are part and parcel of running a large household and managing a successful lace business. Second, between 1860 and 1877, Zélie endured an unremitting succession of births and deaths. During these years, Zélie bore the deaths of both of her parents, a sister, her father-in-law, and four of her children. The deaths of her first two children—Joseph-Louis, age five months, and Joseph-Jean-Baptiste, age eight months—filled Zélie with dread that her other children would suffer a similar fate.

When Zélie was pregnant with Céline (1869), she wrote to her sister-in-law Céline Guérin, "You would not believe how afraid I am, when I think of the little baby that I am awaiting. I imagine that it will be the same as the other two, and it becomes like a constant nightmare for me."[9] For the next several years, this nightmare of foreboding anxiety and grief engulfed Zélie.

Less than a year after Céline was born, Zélie became pregnant again (Mélanie-Thérèse). A month into this pregnancy,

Zélie's beloved five-and-a-half-year-old daughter Hélène died. Zélie was devastated. She became absorbed in her loss. She wrote to Isidore: "Since I lost this child, I experience an intense desire to see her once more. . . . There is not a moment of the day when I am not thinking of her" (S 3). To add to Zélie's grief, Mélanie-Thérèse died two months after she was born.

Seventeen months after Mélanie-Thérèse died, Zélie became pregnant with Thérèse. At this time, Zélie wrote: "I have nightmares about this every night. However, I must have hope that I shall come out better than I believe and shall not have the grief of losing it" (L 1198). Although Thérèse was safely brought to term, Zélie's anxiety did not subside. For months, she continued to be consumed with worry over Thérèse's fragile health. "I am extremely worried with regard to my little Thérèse. . . . Will I have to lose this one?" (January 17, 1873) (L 1200). "I have no hope whatever of saving her" (March 1, 1873) (L 1201). "I am busy and so unhappy for the past two weeks that I have no rest day or night . . . I fear losing her" (March 9, 1873) (L 1202). "Since I wrote you, I have had many sorrows; my little daughter was getting worse and worse. . . . all the gravest signs that preceded the death of my other little angels were evident" (March 16, 1873) (L 1203–4).

Compounding Zélie's anxiety during this time was her constant worry about her older daughter Léonie (nine years old), a child who was mentally slow and emotionally unstable. Her frequent outbursts of anger were a concern and an embarrassment to the whole family. Zélie tried to put Léonie in a boarding school, but Léonie was refused admittance because of her disruptive personality. However, in January 1874, Léonie was accepted, but only on a trial basis. Three months later, when it looked as if Léonie would be sent home, Zélie wrote to Isidore, "If she is sent back to me I will be in despair. My only hope is to leave her there for years."¹⁰ This hope was dashed in June when Léonie was sent home. "As you can imagine," Zélie wrote to her sister-in-law, "this has vexed me terribly: more than that, the pain that it has caused me is with me constantly. . . . When she is with the other [children], she loses all her self-control and becomes terribly unruly."¹¹ Thérèse was subjected to Léonie's outbursts. Three months prior to Léonie being sent home from boarding school, Thérèse had returned from Rose's farm.

Zélie's emotional state, which was the result of her melancholic temperament, the stress of raising her family, running a business, the death of her children and loved ones, her worry over Léonie, and her despair over her impending death (Zélie was diagnosed with inoperable breast cancer) created an extremely anxious world for Thérèse. This is because a mother's emotions are contagious. As psychiatrist Harry Stack Sullivan wrote, "The tension of anxiety when present in the mothering one induces anxiety in the infant."¹²

The overall effect of breathing an anxious atmosphere early in life is that it permeates the psyche with a formless fear that makes the child chronically apprehensive that something dreadful is about to happen. Because of past separation experiences, Thérèse's apprehension was that her mother would abandon her. It is within this perspective that we can begin to understand why the death of Zélie had such a profound impact upon Thérèse's personality. It is a great trauma for any child to experience the death of her mother, but *how much more* traumatic was it for Thérèse because of previous separations? On August 28, 1877, when Thérèse was four years old, her worst nightmare became a reality. Zélie died.

One way of understanding the change that took place in Thérèse at the time of Zélie's death is to view it as an intensification and extension of the change that had already taken place before Zélie died. Just as Thérèse had clung to her mother, now she clung to her family. Just as Thérèse could not endure being outside her mother's presence, now she could not endure being outside of the presence of her family. "I could not bear the company of strangers and found my joy only within the intimacy of the family" (S 35). We can only risk leaving home if we have the assurance that home will still be there when we return. Emotionally, Thérèse did not have this assurance.

Thérèse exhibited what the literature calls a childhood avoidant personality disorder. Its primary traits are "persistent and excessive shrinking from stranger contact; a desire for affection and acceptance, and a generally warm relationship with family members; and distancing behavior that interferes with social/peer relationships . . . and apprehensiveness in new situations and unfamiliar surroundings."[13]

Are we any different than Thérèse? Do we not all have an "avoidant personality," in the sense that we expend an enormous amount of energy in the service of allaying our fears in the attempt to feel secure? Like Thérèse, we all seek security by staying within the circle of the familiar and become anxious when we perceive that the boundaries of the predictable have been breached. Like Thérèse, we are afraid of being overwhelmed by the strangeness of life and are terrified that someday we will encounter a reality beyond our power to cope. Even though *what* makes us anxious and *how* we barricade ourselves against our fears may differ widely from Thérèse, we all share the desire to avoid anxiety and feel secure.

Like Thérèse, the events in our childhood have deeply shaped our emotional lives. Seemingly small events will trigger enormous amounts of fear or anger. Events that are "small in appearance" cause us to "suffer intensely" (S 160). We should never be surprised at the depth of our emotions in the face of daily events. For years I felt that I was a child masquerading as an adult because many life situations that others seemed to take in stride filled me with anxiety and dread. Once I remember saying to myself, "I just don't feel like an adult." As I heard myself say these words, I asked myself the question, "What does it mean to *feel* like an adult?" Rachel, a young girl on her eleventh birthday, in Sandra Cisneros' short story *Eleven,* gives us an answer to this question.

> What they don't understand about birthdays and what they never tell you is that when you're eleven, you're also ten, and nine, and eight, and seven, and six, and five, and four, and three, and two, and one. And when you wake up on your eleventh birthday you expect to feel eleven, but you don't. You open your eyes and everything's just like yesterday, only its today. And you don't feel eleven at all. You feel like you're still ten. And you are ten underneath the year that makes you eleven. Like some days you might say something stupid, and that's the part of you that's still ten. Or maybe some days you might need to sit on your mama's lap because you're scared, and that's the part of you that's five. And maybe one day when you're all grown up maybe you will need to cry like if you're three. That's what I tell Mama when she's sad and needs to cry. Maybe she's feeling three. Because the way you grow old is kind of like an onion or like the rings inside a tree trunk or like my little wooden dolls that fit one inside the other, each year inside the next one.[14]

What does it mean to *feel* like an adult? Some days it feels like the deep separation anxiety of a one-year-old; on other days it feels like the savage rage of a two-year-old; and on still other days it feels like the nail biting envy of a three-year-old.

Becoming an adult does not mean that the deep emotional wounds of childhood disappear. Rather, being an adult means *choosing* to make courageous decisions in the face of powerful emotions. We have an example of this when Thérèse was appointed novice mistress. "When I was given the office of entering into the sanctuary of souls, I saw immediately that the task was beyond my strength. I threw myself into the arms of God as a little child and, hiding my face in His hair, I said: 'Lord, I am too little to nourish Your children; if You wish to give through me what is suitable for each, fill my little hand and without leaving Your arms or turning my head, I shall give Your treasures to the soul who will come and ask for nourishment'" (S 237–38).

Thérèse's reaction is all too human. When she was assigned a job that she thought was too much for her to handle, she felt overwhelmed, incompetent, unqualified, and inadequate. Thérèse felt like a frightened child clinging to her father, the same feelings she had experienced when she clung to her mother and her family.

However, Thérèse does not *apologize* for her fears. She does not berate herself for feeling like a child; rather her fears and insecurities are the *context* within which she places her trust in God. It is as if Thérèse is saying to all of us, "There are many situations in life that trigger the deep-seated fears of childhood. I have come to see that this is a normal part of daily life. I have also come to understand that our childhood wounds are not obstacles to our spiritual growth but are in some mysterious manner the path on which we find our way back to God. The deep-seated fears of my life have forced me to abandon my self-sufficiency and to rely upon the grace of God."

A Nurturing and Healing Atmosphere

ON HER DEATHBED, Zélie gave her last look neither to her husband nor any of her children but to her sister-in-law Céline Guérin. "I believed I understood that look," Céline Guérin wrote to Thérèse, "which nothing will be able to make me forget. It is engraved within my heart. Since that day, I have tried to replace her whom God had taken away from you, but, alas! nothing can replace a mother!" (L 745). Céline Guérin understood that Zélie was asking her to take care of her children. The Guérins took this request very seriously. Isidore Guérin was named the deputy guardian of the Martin children, and he proposed to the Martins that they move to Lisieux where the Guérins lived. The Martins agreed.

The move to Lisieux proved to be a good one for the Martin family. Both *Story of a Soul* and the family correspondence paint an idyllic picture of the Martin family during its early years in Lisieux. Thérèse's account of herself during this time gives the impression that they were some of the happiest years of her life. The whole atmosphere that surrounded the Martin family in Lisieux was much more joyous and serene than that which had surrounded them in Alençon. What made the difference? There is no *single* factor that accounts for this change, for a psychic atmosphere, like a physical one, is composed of many particles. Let us explore some of the elements that constituted the new atmosphere that the Martin family enjoyed in Lisieux.

Les Buissonnets. Before the Martin family arrived in Lisieux, Isidore had procured a spacious, well-lighted house for them to rent. It was cloistered by a ring of trees and walls and sequestered on the outskirts of town. "From the house, you are not seen from any direction," Isidore wrote to Louis, "and you see no road but simply a delightful panorama of the town" (L 128). The beauty of the grounds added to this contemplative atmosphere. "It is a charming house, cheerful and gay," wrote Marie to her father, "with a large garden in which Céline and Thérèse will be able to play" (L 130). Their new home, which was promptly christened Les Buissonnets ("little bushes") by the Martin children because little bushes surrounded the house, was adjacent to a beautiful spacious park, *Le jardin de l'Etoile*, which was a source of sheer delight for Thérèse. "This baby loves flowers so much . . . she's very soon going to pick all there are of lilies of the valley in the *jardin de l'Etoile*" (L 135). Thérèse, who was at heart a country girl, and who was deeply nourished by the beauty of nature, came home to herself at Les Buissonnets.

Not only was Les Buissonnets sequestered from prying eyes, so was the Martin family. Except for church functions, the Martins rarely participated in the social life of Lisieux. Most evenings were spent quietly at home gathered around the family hearth listening to Louis either singing, reading from Dom Guéranger's *The Liturgical Year,* or reciting "from memory long passages [of poetry] principally from Lamartine and Victor Hugo."[15]

The peaceful, bucolic atmosphere that permeated Les Buissonnets was in stark contrast to the noisy, urban atmosphere that had surrounded the Martin household in Alençon. Their house in Alençon opened on to a busy city street and was a thoroughfare for customers and employees associated with

Zélie's lace business. Because their living space was also a place of employment, privacy and silence were at a premium.

The Absence of Zélie. My father, who was an alcoholic, died when I was a freshman in high school. I didn't feel either sad or happy. I felt an incredible sense of relief. I no longer had to hold my breath waiting for the next shameful incident to occur. The relief I felt is neither a commentary on my father's love for me nor a judgment upon myself as his son; it was simply a natural reaction to a source of shame being removed from my life. Similarly, Thérèse could have also felt relief as the result of Zélie's absence, for Zélie's love for Thérèse could not shield Thérèse from her anxiety. Nor could Thérèse's love for her mother protect her from ingesting it. Psychologist Stephen A. Mitchell presents the following scenario:

> Consider a devoted caregiver who is worried about something altogether unrelated to the baby. The baby picks up the anxiety and experiences it as a tension, demanding relief. He cries in the same way he responds to tensions created by various needs for satisfaction. The caregiver moves toward the baby, concerned and hoping to comfort him. But as she moves closer in her effort to soothe, the caregiver also brings her own anxiety closer to the baby.
>
> Most likely she is even more anxious now, precisely because of the baby's distress. The closer she gets, the more anxious the baby becomes. Unless the caregiver can find a way to pull both herself and the baby out of their anxious state, the baby experiences a snowballing tension with no possible relief. When the infant is anxious, she is unable to feed, to cuddle, to sleep.[16]

This may have been the situation between Thérèse and Zélie. Thérèse would not nurse from Zélie, which was thought to be the result of enteritis (an inflammation of Thérèse's intestinal tract). However, Thérèse fed from Rose almost immediately. Zélie wrote to her sister-in-law the following account:

> "We [Rose and I] left [Rose's farm] after half an hour and we reached my home at ten-thirty. . . . I went quickly up to my room . . . I did not know if I should go down, but I decided to do so. And what did I see? The child was sucking wholeheartedly, and did not give up until one o'clock in the afternoon. . . . my little Thérèse opened her eyes and began to smile. From that moment she was totally cured; her healthy appearance returned and her gaiety as well." (L 1204)

When Zélie was absent, the snowballing cycle of anxiety was broken. Thérèse could relax in Rose's arms and began to nurse.

Not only was Zélie unaware of the negative impact that her emotional state was having upon Thérèse, but it was also beyond her control. Zélie did not choose her mother who "was very severe" with her and made her "childhood and youth . . . as dismal as a winding sheet" (S 2). Nor did she have any control over the death of her four children, Léonie's troubled personality, or her breast cancer, all of which contributed to her anxious state. Zélie could not protect Thérèse from her anxiety. Is there any wonder why Zélie's death, while being a great loss for Thérèse, was not also a source of relief?

Zélie was a loving mother and a holy woman (the Church canonized her in 2015), but even saints are not exempt from the woundedness of the human condition. Zélie, like every parent, could not protect her child from herself. Even when we believe we are doing what is best for our children, we can do them harm. How many parents have disciplined their children with the best intentions that resulted in the worst consequences? Who hasn't, in one form or another, awakened too late to "the awareness of things ill done and done to others' harm which once you took for exercise of virtue"?[17]

So often in life we are oblivious to the pain we inflict upon others. For example, Marie and Pauline were unaware of the suffering they caused Thérèse by not paying attention to her during family visits to Pauline at Carmel. "If I had only known that my poor little Thérèse," writes Marie, "had suffered so much from this! I was far from suspecting it. However, I remember one day how she said to you: 'Look Pauline, I'm wearing the little skirt that you made for me.' We hardly paid any attention to her childish prattle, and, afterward, I saw tears in her eyes" (L 151). Pauline shared the same regret: "I was unaware of the abyss of sadness that formed in her [Thérèse's] soul at my departure. I understand very well now how the five minutes given to her with me [at the end of the visits] could only cause her more anguish. . . . If I had only known!" (L 151).

"If I had only known, if I had only known, if I had only known" is the regret-filled lament that we all share as blind human beings. This is not remorse and guilt that follows in the wake of having *consciously* inflicted pain upon another, but the sorrow that afflicts us when we realize that we have unintentionally contributed to another's pain. In the midst of our sorrow, we need to make our own the words of our merciful God as he hung upon the cross, "Father forgive them for they *know not* what they do."

Léonie. Another factor that made the atmosphere at Les Buissonnets less stressful for Thérèse was that, two months after the Martin family moved to Lisieux, Léonie became a boarder at the local school run by Benedictine nuns. As a result of Léonie's absence, the Martin household was more peaceful. This is not a judgment upon Léonie—it is merely a fact of which Léonie herself was painfully aware. As an adult, Léonie wrote to Pauline. "My childhood was dreadful, disfiguring our beautiful and holy family. How merciful God has been to me!"[18]

The Guérins. Thérèse's Aunt Céline and Uncle Isidore along with their children Jeanne and Marie (who became Thérèse's playmates) were important people who contributed to the positive atmosphere of Thérèse's life at Les Buissonnets. Thérèse was very much at home in the Guérin household, which was only "seven hundred and sixty-four paces" from Les Buissonnets (L 128).

When Thérèse was five, her father took Marie and Pauline to Paris for an Exposition. During this time, Léonie and Céline stayed at the Benedictine school, and Thérèse stayed by herself at the Guérins'. Céline Guérin wrote to the Martins while they were in Paris: "Thérèse isn't in the least bit bored, and she seems to be very much at home with her aunt" (L 131). This observation coincides with Thérèse's own experience. She wrote, "Marie Guérin is at the country since Monday, but I'm enjoying myself all alone with Aunt" (L 133).

But what about uncle Isidore? The image that many people have of him is that of a gruff old man. This image is based upon a single event that is recorded in *Story of a Soul.* "I was very much frightened when he placed me on his knee and sang Blue Beard in a formidable tone of voice" (S 42). This passage should be interpreted in context. First, immediately before this incident, Thérèse wrote, "I listened with great pleasure to all Uncle had to say" (S 42). Second, the "Blue Beard" incident seems to be saying more about Thérèse's temperament than it does about her uncle. After all, Thérèse is comparing her experience of being bounced up and down on her uncle's knee and sung in a *formidable tone of voice* a song about a man who murders his wives to her experience of sitting on the knee of her father, who "used to sing, in his *beautiful voice,* airs that filled the soul with *profound thoughts*" (S 43, emphases added).

It is also worth noting that Thérèse wrote the following at the age of ten and a half regarding the time that she spent convalescing in the Guérin household during her mysterious illness: "Friends of the family came to visit me . . . but I begged Marie to tell them I wanted no visits. . . . The only visit I liked was that of Uncle and Aunt" (S 63).

Louis Martin. Perhaps the single most important factor that contributed to the healing atmosphere at Les Buissonnets was the *predictable availability* of Thérèse's father. In Alençon, Louis Martin was not available to his children (either physically or mentally) as much as he wished. This was because much of his time and energy was consumed by Zélie's illness and her lace business. He was in charge of the business's financial records and was frequently away from home obtaining orders and making deliveries. But after Zélie's death, all of this changed. Louis sold the lace business, invested the proceeds, and settled into a quiet life that was comprised of prayer, spiritual reading, gardening, fishing, making pilgrimages, and tending to the needs of his children.

This was a crucial factor in Thérèse's new life; it gave her the security of predictability.

> As soon as my classes were over [Thérèse was taught at home by her older sisters until she was eight], I climbed up to the belvédère and showed my badge and my marks to Papa. . . . Each afternoon I took a walk with Papa. We made our visit to the Blessed Sacrament together, going to a different church

each day. . . . After the walk (during which Papa bought me a little present worth a few sous) we returned to the house. . . . It was a great joy for me to prepare mixtures with little seeds and pieces of bark I found on the ground, and I'd bring them to Papa in a pretty little cup. Poor Papa stopped all his work and with a smile he pretended to drink. (S 36)

His predictable, approachable, and lovingly attentive presence was a major factor that shaped Thérèse's image of God, a God she could approach with *confidence*.

The predictable availability of Thérèse's father, coupled with the maternal care of her sisters, the loving presence of her aunt and uncle, the beauty of nature that surrounded Les Buissonnets, and the absence of Zélie's anxious presence *combined* to form a nurturing and healing atmosphere that Thérèse needed at this fragile period in her life. There is much for us to ponder here.

All of us contribute to the atmosphere of the world around us by what we say and do. There is a very touching scene in Charles Dickens's story *A Christmas Carol* where the Ghost of Christmas Past escorts Scrooge to a time when Scrooge was apprenticed to a kindly old man named Fezziwig. As Scrooge gazes upon Fezziwig, he begins to recover a deep sense of joy that he had once felt in the presence of his former master. Scrooge says of Fezziwig that he had "the power to render us happy or unhappy, to make our service light or burdensome, a pleasure or a toil. Say that his power lies in words and looks, in things so slight and insignificant that it is impossible to add and count 'em up; what then? The happiness he gives is quite as great as if it cost a fortune."[19] There was no *single* deed or *great* act that Fezziwig did that created an atmosphere of joy among his employees, but *seemingly* insignificant particles of behavior, words, looks, and small acts of kindness that *together* created a congenial atmosphere that made their labor light and pleasurable. The same can be said for each of us.

Thomas Hardy once said that every person is like a planet who carries around in his or her orbit their own atmosphere. What happens when people come into my orbit? By my words, looks, gestures, and deeds, what atmosphere do I create at home or in the workplace? If there is anything that I have learned in the past forty years in religious life, it is this: each member in the community is a very powerful person who has the capacity to make the common life a joy or a burden. If the atmosphere of a community, marriage, or place of employment is suffused with what Wordsworth calls the "best portion of a good man's life; / His little, nameless, unremembered acts / Of kindness and love," then that place will be joyful; if these qualities are absent, it will not.[20]

It is by our little, nameless, unremembered acts of kindness and love that we diffuse the fragrance of God's presence in the world about us and prove our love for God. "I have no other means of proving my love for you [my God] than that of strewing flowers, that is, not allowing one little sacrifice to escape, not one look, one word, profiting by all the smallest things and doing them through love" (S 196). The same is true for us.

The Halcyon Days of Youth

It was within the atmosphere that surrounded Les Buissonnets that Thérèse's deeply contemplative soul found fertile soil to grow.

> They were beautiful days for me, those days when my "dear King" took me fishing with him. I was very fond of the countryside, flowers, birds, etc. Sometimes I would try to fish . . . but I preferred to go *alone* and sit down on the grass bedecked with flowers, and then my thoughts became very profound indeed! Without knowing what it was to meditate, my soul was absorbed in real prayer. I listened to distant sounds, the murmuring of the wind, etc. At times, the indistinct notes of some military music reached me where I was, filling my heart with a sweet melancholy. Earth then seemed to be a place of exile and I could dream only of heaven.
>
> The afternoon sped by quickly and soon we had to return to Les Buissonnets. Before leaving, I would take the lunch I had brought in my little basket. The *beautiful* bread and jam you had prepared had changed its appearance: instead of the lively colors it had earlier, I now saw only a light rosy tint and the bread had become old and crumbled. Earth again seemed a sad place and I understood that in heaven alone joy will be without any clouds. (S 37)

This passage gives us a glimpse into two important aspects of Thérèse's spiritual life in its incipient stage: first, the relationship of nature and beauty in the formation of her image of God and how it functioned in her spiritual life; second, her consciousness of the transitoriness of life.

The Relationship of Nature and Beauty in the Formation of Thérèse's Image of God and how it Functioned in her Spiritual Life. Images taken from nature abound in Thérèse's writings, especially images of flowers. In some way this is unfortunate because they give a sentimental cast to her thought, and erroneously communicate that her floral metaphors are nothing but window dressing to her spirituality. This is not true, for the images and metaphors that we consistently use to structure our thought patterns express our innermost selves.

Psychologists tell us that the experiences of our early life, especially the first year of life, lay the foundation of our conception of reality. In this regard, we need to recall that the first year of Thérèse's life was spent on Rose's farm. Thus, we can assume that many of Thérèse's earliest experiences that were deeply impressed upon the template of her memory were those of nature. And if we can believe what was said of Thérèse during this year, namely that she was a happy child, then her experiences of nature became inseparably fused with joy and happiness. This is a significant fact about Thérèse's inner life because our earliest memories shape the lenses through which we experience life.

Our earliest memories are not merely specific events of our childhood that we can recall to our conscious mind, but, more importantly, the distillation of all the experiences of our infancy that form, in Alfred Adler's words, our "emotional tone or state of mind."[21] The inner atmosphere that is formed by memory is the emotionally colored lens through which we apprehend life; as Wordsworth puts it, our "first affections, those shadowy recollections, are yet the fountain light of all our day, are yet a master light of all our seeing."[22]

We will never know for certain what part the early experiences of nature's beauty contributed to the fountain light of Thérèse's vision of reality, but we do have indications that they were deeply embedded in her psyche. For example, in Thérèse's play *Joan of Arc and her Mission*, she puts into the mouth of Joan of Arc as she lies in prison her own yearnings for nature's beauty that she experienced in childhood and was deprived of in Carmel. "Never again shall I see the places of childhood, the meadow laughing in its floral radiance. Never again gaze on the distant mountains, the silvery peaks, dipped deep in cerulean blue. Never again hear the trembling vesper bells breathing sweet dreams through the pure breezes. . . . Here when I fall asleep amid my tears, I dream of scents, of the sweet morning dew, and dream of the magic of woods and vale and fields but roughly the clank of my chains awakens me."[23] Likewise, Thérèse tells us that her dreams were "usually about such things as woods, flowers, streams, and the sea; I see beautiful children almost all the time; I catch butterflies and birds the like of which I've never seen before" (S 170–71).

Throughout her writings, Thérèse uses the sun as an image of God's presence. For example, in the opening pages of *Story of a Soul,* where Thérèse compares souls to different types of flowers, God is symbolized as the sun who gazes down lovingly upon us. "Just as the sun shines simultaneously on the tall cedars and on each little flower as though it were alone on the earth, so our Lord is occupied particularly with each soul as though there were no others like it" (S 14). This image is central to Thérèse's spirituality because it symbolizes her image of God as a loving God who not only gazes down upon us with love in our loveliness, but also a God who gazes down upon us with mercy in our sinfulness. "And yet, after all these misdeeds, instead of going and hiding away in a corner, to weep over its misery and to die of sorrow, the little bird turns towards its beloved Sun, presenting its wet wings to its beneficent rays. It cries like a swallow and in its sweet song it recounts in detail all its infidelities, thinking in the boldness of its full trust that it will acquire in even greater fullness the love of *Him* who came to call not the just but sinners" (S 198–99). Thérèse's experiences of nature's beauty that shaped her image of God also aided her in doing God's will. Let us consider two examples.

When Thérèse was five years old, her father brought her to the seaside town of Tourville, where she saw the ocean for the first time.

> Never will I forget the impression the sea made upon me . . . everything spoke to my soul of God's grandeur and power. . . . In the evening at that moment when the sun seems to bathe itself in the immensity of the waves, leaving a *luminous trail* behind, I went and sat down on the huge rock with *Pauline.* Then I recalled the touching story of the "Golden Trail." I contemplated this luminous trail for a long time. It was to me the image of God's grace shedding its light across the path the little white-sailed vessel had to travel. And near Pauline, I made the resolution never to wander far away from the glance of Jesus in order to travel peacefully toward the eternal shore. (S 48-49)[24]

Thérèse's experience of the ocean could have been only an aesthetically pleasing experience. But it was more than that. She brought it into the inner chamber of her will and made a resolution to stay close to God. She fused together in her mind her desire to do good with an experience of beauty. We see something similar in Thérèse's experience of the grandeur of the Alps on her trip to Rome.

When I saw all these beauties very profound thoughts came to life in my soul. I seemed to understand already the grandeur of God and the marvels of heaven. The religious life appeared to me *exactly as it is* with its *subjections,* its small sacrifices carried out in the shadows.

I understood how easy it is to become all wrapped up in self, forgetting entirely the sublime goal of one's calling. I said to myself: When I am a prisoner in Carmel and trials come my way and I have only a tiny bit of the starry heavens to contemplate, I shall remember what my eyes have seen today. This thought will encourage me and I shall easily forget my own little interests, recalling the grandeur and power of God, this God whom I want to love alone. I shall not have the misfortune of snatching after *straws,* now that "*my HEART HAS AN IDEA of what Jesus has reserved for those who love him.*" (S 125–26)

These are two examples of what the American psychologist William James recommends as ways in which we should relate to aesthetic experiences. "[Never] have an emotion at a concert, without expressing it afterward in *some* active way. Let the expression be the least thing in the world—speaking genially to one's grandmother, or giving up one's seat in a horse car, if nothing more heroic offers itself but let it not fail to take place."[25]

If we fail to link our experiences of beauty to goodness, then aesthetic experiences can degenerate into mere sentimentality and insulate us from life instead of connecting us to it. In this regard, James speaks of "the weeping of a Russian lady over the fictitious personages in a play, while her coachman is freezing to death on his seat outside."[26] The woman is so absorbed in her emotions that she has become blind and insensitive to the world around her; she is so touched by the characters in the play that she is out of touch with real life.

The Beautiful (Gk. *to kalon*) derived from the Greek verb *kaleo* means to beckon or to call. Beauty is evocative; it evokes our deepest desire for happiness and fulfillment because beauty is a manifestation of the source of our being—God. "The beauty of the creature," writes St. Thomas, "is nothing else than the likeness of the divine beauty participated in things."[27] The purpose of beauty is to draw us *to* God, but it can also draw us *away from* God if we become *attached* to the *experience* of beauty. St. John of the Cross tells us that some people "let themselves be encumbered by the very consolations and favors God bestows on them for the sake of their advancing, and they advance not at all" (A Prol 7).

Aesthetic experiences are consolations to which we can become addicted. The "aesthetic" personality, as treated by Kierkegaard, is a sobering portrait of the spiritual impoverishment that ensues when a person's main stance toward life is seeking pleasurable experiences. The desire for aesthetically pleasing experiences in such individuals often masks an inner dread of the mundane and a deep restlessness and ennui of spirit. Such people crave the *intensity* of experience as a means of assuaging boredom and the deep despair of inner emptiness. And because aesthetic experiences are akin to religious experiences, one can easily counterfeit the other. We see an example of this in Flaubert's character Emma Bovary.

> She gently succumbed to the mystical languor induced by the perfumes of the altar, the coolness of the holy-water fonts, the gleaming of the candles. Instead of following the Mass she kept her prayer book open at the holy pictures with their sky-blue borders. . . . When she went to confession she invented small sins in order to linger on her knees in the darkness, her hands joined, her face at the grille, the priest

whispering just above her. The metaphors constantly used in sermons—"betrothed," "spouse," "heavenly lover," "mystical marriage"—excited her in a thrilling new way. . . . She had to extract a kind of personal advantage from things; and she rejected as useless everything that promised no immediate gratification—for her temperament was more sentimental than artistic, and what she was looking for was emotions.[28]

Madame Bovary is a symbol of a life of will-less affectation, a person who has divorced the sensual from the spiritual, who seduces the sensual instead of heeding the beckoning of the Beautiful. She does not grasp that the immanent beauty of creation adumbrates the transcendent beauty of God, that it is an aperture through which we glimpse the Eternal that in turn awakens our desire to see God. As St. John of the Cross writes: "The soul, wounded with love through a trace of the beauty of her Beloved, which she has known *through* creatures, [is] anxious to see the invisible beauty" (C 6.1, emphasis added).

Because of personal differences, each of us is touched more deeply by certain traces of God's beauty than by others. For some people, nature is the supreme sacrament of Divine Beauty. Others encounter Beauty through one of the nine Muses of the arts or through one of the sciences. Many scientists have experienced the reality expressed in Keats's assertion that "Beauty is truth, truth Beauty."[29] "Mathematics," wrote Bertrand Russell, "rightly viewed, possesses not only truth, but supreme beauty—a beauty cold and austere," or, as Edna St. Vincent Millay wrote, "Euclid alone has looked on beauty bare."[30] Johannes Kepler compared the symmetry of the laws that govern the orbits of the planets to "the harmony of contrapuntal music."[31] And physicist Richard Feynman marvels that nature obeys "such an elegant and simple law as this law of gravitation."[32]

God who is "infinitely elegant" (A 1.4.4), to use St. John of the Cross's phrase, is encountered by all of us through the manifold works of creation. It is beneficial to employ those aspects of creation that most deeply speak to us of God's presence, for they are actual graces in our lives. St. Teresa of Ávila, in *The Way of Perfection*, recommended to her sisters as an aid to prayer "to carry about an image or painting of this Lord that is *to your liking*, not so as to carry it about on your heart and never look at it but so as to speak often with Him; for He will *inspire you*" (W 26.9, emphases added). Teresa's advice to use what personally speaks to us of God's presence can be extended to include anything that is communicated through the senses, be it a poem, a verse of Scripture, a piece of music, etc. It may be even a memory as it was for Thérèse who recalled the beauty of the Alps in order to restore her perspective on life. But whatever we use, the essential question that we must ask ourselves is whether it helps us *to love*. The Beautiful cannot be divorced from the True and the Good; they are three inseparable attributes of God. Thus, Infinite Beauty mirrored in creation beckons us, as it did Thérèse, to *choose* that which is True and Good.

The Eternal and the Transitoriness of Life. "The *beautiful* bread and jam you had prepared had changed its appearance: instead of the lively colors it had earlier, I now saw only a light rosy tint and the bread had become old and crumbled. Earth again seemed a sad place and I understood that in heaven alone joy will be without any clouds" (S 37). This passage reveals the precocious consciousness of Thérèse. How many children her age (Thérèse was between five and seven) when looking upon a faded jelly sandwich would begin to reflect upon the transitoriness of life?

As a child, Thérèse was reflective far beyond her years. She possessed a deeply contemplative soul that saw all things in the light of eternity. One day when Thérèse was eleven, one of her teachers at the Benedictine boarding school asked her what she did on her free afternoons when she was alone. Thérèse said, "I went behind my bed in an empty space which was there, and that it was easy to close myself in with my bedcurtain and that '*I thought.*' 'But what do you think about?' she asked. 'I think about God, about life, about ETERNITY'" (S 74). At a tender age, Thérèse possessed what Wordsworth called "the faith that looks through death / In years that bring the philosophic mind."[33]

Thérèse's faith that looked through death was neither morbid nor escapist, but the backdrop of her vision of life upon which she was able to see all things in perspective. It formed within her the paradoxical perspective that, since all things are passing, there is nothing in this life that is of ultimate significance, but simultaneously, because life is short, and our time on this earth is limited, there is nothing more important than the choices that we make in time, for they determine our existence for all eternity. "In Homer's *Odyssey*," writes Rabbi Harold Kushner, "there is a passage in which Ulysses meets Calypso [an immortal sea goddess]. She is fascinated by Ulysses, never having met a mortal before. As we read on, we come to realize that Calypso envies Ulysses because he will not live forever. His life becomes more full of meaning, his every decision is more significant, precisely because his time is limited, and what he chooses to do with it represents a real choice."[34]

The scarcity of time confers value upon every choice that we make in the one, unrepeatable life that God has given us. "I expect to pass through this world but once," as the old saying goes. "Therefore, if there is any kindness that I can show or any good that I can do, let me do it now and not defer it to another time. For I shall not pass this way again." Each of us has been assigned to live in this world at a unique juncture of time, space, and circumstance that has not been entrusted to anyone else. Our vocation during our brief sojourn on this earth is to love the people whom God has commended to our care. Seeing time against the backdrop of eternity helped Thérèse to shape a clear vision of life. Her abiding sense of death did not distance her from daily life but helped her to focus on what was truly essential in it.

Thérèse believed that a mindful remembrance of death is a powerful antidote to not becoming absorbed in the passing things of this world. "The friends we had [at Alençon] were too worldly; they knew too well how to ally the joys of this earth to the service of God. They didn't think about *death* enough, and yet *death* had paid its visit to a great number of those whom I knew, the young, the rich, the happy" (S 73). Thérèse makes a distinction here between being merely cognizant of the fact of death and pondering mortality to such a degree that it has an emotional impact upon our consciousness.

One of the ways that Thérèse deepened her consciousness of the transitoriness of all things was to "cast a glance on the past" (S 15). "I love to return in spirit to the *enchanting* places where they [the friends of the Martin family at Alençon] lived, wondering where these people are, what became of their houses and gardens where I saw them enjoy life's luxuries? And I see that all is vanity and vexation of spirit under the sun" (S 73). Here, Thérèse is not simply reflecting upon what happened to *other* people but rather is looking back at *herself* and considering the person she might have become. For Thérèse tells us that she was attracted and "easily dazzled" by the social life at Alençon, which "had its charms for [her]." She "consider[ed] it a great grace not to have remained at Alençon" (S 73). Thérèse is looking back at herself over the distance of a decade, on the person she might have become if she had stayed in Alençon. Such a realization was a moment of grace.

In the *Paradiso,* as Dante is nearing the end of his journey, he stands with his beloved Beatrice on Saturn, the highest planetary heaven. Beatrice tells Dante that, as his final preparation to enter the presence of God, he must ponder his past by looking down upon the earth.

> My eyes went back through the seven spheres below,
> and I saw this globe, so small, so lost in space,
> I had to smile at such a sorry show . . .
> I saw the dusty little threshing ground
> that makes us ravenous for our mad sins.[35]

In his younger years, Dante had become embroiled in the infighting of Florentine politics. At the time, Florence was the center of his world, but as Dante is reaching his journey's end (Dante died shortly after he wrote the *Paradiso*), he could look back upon that time in his life and recognize his blindness. How often have our minds looked back upon our own little threshing ground where we see ourselves pushing an agenda, defending our point of view tooth and nail, or waging a crusade over an issue that in hindsight seems insignificant and even ridiculous? These realizations are moments of grace.

When we cast a glance upon our past with the haunting question, "What might have been?" we can feel regret and remorse, but we can also experience gratitude and a deep sigh of relief, for each of us has our personal Alençon. Where would I be now if I had not extricated myself from that situation? What would have happened to me if I hadn't had the courage to break off that relationship? How would my life be different if . . . ?

In Charles Dickens's novel *Great Expectations,* after Pip had made a seemingly small decision that eventually changed the whole course of his life, he invites the reader to reflect with him. "That was a memorable day for me, for it made great changes in me. But it is the same with any life. Imagine one selected day struck out of it, and think how different its course would have been. Pause you who read this, and think for a moment of the long chain of iron or gold, of thorns or flowers, that would never have bound you, but for the formation of the first link on one memorable day."[36]

Thérèse paused and meditated upon her life. She knew that it could have turned out far differently than it had, and it could have happened very easily. All she had to do was to take a wrong turn on the road of life and continue to travel down that path. As social reformer Samuel Smiles once said, "Sow a thought and reap an act. Sow an act and reap a habit. Sow a habit and reap a character. Sow a character and reap a destiny." The author of the "little way" who understood that our path leading to God is paved with little acts of love was also keenly aware of how little acts of self-indulgence can imperceptibly lead us away from God.

Meditating upon death helps us to see what is truly important in life and provides perspective that in turn restores a proportionate emotional response to the events of daily life. When we see rightly, we respond reasonably. However, when we are in the grip of either an irresistible impulse or an intense emotion, we cease to *live* in the present moment because we are *absorbed* in it. Paradoxically, we can only live in the present moment if we are conscious of the future, for the things of time can only be clearly seen against the horizon of Eternity. Death, seen in the light of Eternity, illumined all things for Thérèse. "I understand all . . . All passes away. . . . *Death* will pass also, and then we shall enjoy life not for centuries, but millions of years will pass for us like a day, and other millions of years will follow them filled with repose and happiness" (L 709).

In the same way, we become illuminated when we realize that all things pass away. Several years ago, when I was reading on the front porch of our Carmelite retreat house in New Hampshire, I looked up and caught sight of one of my Carmelite brothers walking across the field. He was walking away from the retreat house; his back was stooped and his gait was weary. As I gazed at him, a man many years my senior bathed in the light of the waning day, a poignant sadness came over me at the prospect of his death. "How I will miss him when he is gone," came to my lips, which I repeated over and over to myself.

That morning he and I had a heated argument. But as I looked at him slowly trudging across the field, what we had argued about shrank to its proper insignificance. Because I beheld him bathed in his mortality, I was able to see him in the light of eternity. For the first time in my life, I could perceive a deep goodness in this man, buried beneath a mound of little irritating mannerisms and idiosyncrasies. Learn "to see beneath the surface of circumstances and events," said Thérèse to Céline, and it will prevent you from making rash judgments upon others.[37] This is what Thérèse choose to do. "When I wish to increase this love in me, and when especially the devil tries to place before the eyes of my soul the faults of such and such a sister who is less attractive to me, I hasten to search out her virtues, her good intentions" (S 221).

Seeing beyond the faults of others is not turning a blind eye to them; it is allowing the faults to recede into the background and the goodness to come to the fore. One way to do this is to bathe our neighbor in mortality, for "Death is the mother of beauty."[38] Walter de la Mare bids us to "Look thy last on all things lovely every hour."[39] To do so, we need to look at others as if we were seeing them for the *last time*.

The Distressing Years

THÉRÈSE LIVED A VERY SHELTERED, overprotected existence at Les Buissonnets. Yet that is what she needed to survive those early years immediately following Zélie's death. "Ah! if God had not showered His beneficent *rays* upon His little flower," writes Thérèse, commenting on her family's care after her mother's death, "she could never have accustomed herself to earth, for she was too weak to stand up against the rains and the storms. She needed warmth, a gentle dew, and the springtime breezes" (S 35). Thérèse needed a "hot house" environment in order to survive emotionally. If she had been exposed to the rough and tumble world of other children too soon, and if she had not been treated with kid gloves by her family in the years immediately following the trauma of her mother's death, Thérèse may have remained an infant all of her life.

Paradoxically, Thérèse needed to be "babied" in order to grow up. For if this traumatized child, who could not bear the company of strangers, had been thrown into this strange world too soon and had to fend for herself, she never would have survived. Thérèse's anxiety would have been so great that, in order to protect herself, she would have regressed to an earlier stage of development and may have become fixated there for the rest of her life.

The overprotective environment of Les Buissonnets was a great grace for Thérèse; it provided her with what British psychoanalyst D. W. Winnicott termed a "holding environment," a psychic and physical space within which a child feels protected. But like so many gifts in life, it came with a high price tag attached to it. For when Thérèse eventually had to venture outside the rim of the family circle, she found the adjustment to the world very painful. "The poor little flower had become accustomed to burying her fragile roots in *a chosen soil* made purposely for her. It seemed hard for her to see herself among flowers of all kinds with roots frequently indelicate; and she had to find in this *common soil* the food necessary for her sustenance" (S 53). The *common soil* that Thérèse is referring to was the Benedictine school that she began to attend when she was eight and a half. This was the first time that Thérèse had stepped outside the shelter of her family since Zélie's death.

School Years. Entering school for the first time can be a traumatic experience for any child, for the tasks of adjustment are formidable: the child must grow in independence as he or she separates from family, adapt to a school system and a peer culture, and cultivate the social skills necessary to enter into the world of play. What will often determine how successful a child will be in accomplishing these tasks is his or her previous life experience. If a child has clung too tightly to his or her family and feels secure only within the family circle, then the experience of separation that school entails will be traumatic. Also, if a child has been severely restricted in normal interaction with his or her neighborhood peer group, then adjusting to a new one will make the task more difficult. Furthermore, if a preschooler has not been exposed to the normal range of childhood games or does not have a modicum of skills in these games, then her adjustment to school will be at a distinct disadvantage.[40] Thérèse entered school with a deficiency in all three areas: she was afraid to venture outside her family circle; she was restricted in her interactions with other children; and she lacked the knowledge of both games and play that was normal for a child her age.

"I didn't know how to play like other children and as a consequence wasn't a very pleasant companion" (S 54). "I *didn't know* how to play with dolls" (S 36).

These handicaps generated a negative reaction from Thérèse's peers. The "other girls," says Céline, "finding her ill-adapted to their games, disregarded her. She did try, but she never succeeded in pleasing them. So she suffered a lot from the rude treatment that was meted out to her. From then on, she liked to keep away [from them]."[41] In consequence, Thérèse became isolated from her peers. "In the days of my life as a day boarder . . . I walked sad and sick in the big yard" (S 87). Feeling inadequate in entering into the world of play and being shunned by her peers, Thérèse believed "herself to be inferior to the others," said Céline.[42]

To begin to understand the mental and emotional impact that the behavior and attitude of Thérèse's peers had upon her, two things must be kept in mind. First, when Thérèse entered school, she was *already withdrawn* and had a fragile sense of self-worth. "From the time she was four and a half . . . it was as if a veil had been drawn over all the fine qualities which the Lord had bestowed on her. Her school-mistresses recognized her intelligence, but in the world she was considered incompetent and stupid. This opinion was caused chiefly by her excessive shyness: it made her indecisive and had a paralyzing effect on her in everything."[43] Second, what deepened Thérèse's isolation was that she kept her thoughts and feelings to herself; she didn't share them with anyone, even her family. All of Thérèse's siblings testified at her beatification process that they did not know what Thérèse was going through until many years later. Thérèse's reticence to share her pain was a trait that had been formed in her at an early age. "[I] got into the habit of not complaining ever" (S 30).

Even though suffering in silence was a virtue in Thérèse as a mature adult, we should not presuppose that it was a sign of virtue in her as an eight-and-a-half-year-old child. Thérèse may have had the right intention to suffer in silence, namely, not to be a burden to her family, but her decision to do so may have lacked the prudence that she acquired in later years. We need to read *Story of a Soul* with intelligence and interpret the events of Thérèse's life within context, so that we do not canonize every action of this canonized saint.

The overall impact that Thérèse's silence had upon her may be summed up in one sentence by Céline. "She bore all without complaining, but it depressed her."[44] Before Thérèse entered boarding school, she exhibited symptoms of anaclitic or childhood depression, which is usually the result of being separated from one's mother. "These infants," writes psychologist René Spitz, "develop a weepy behavior that is in marked contrast to their previously happy and outgoing behavior. After a time this weepiness gives way to withdrawal."[45] This description mirrors the change that took place in Thérèse as a result of Zélie's death. "My happy disposition completely changed after Mama's death. I, once so full of life, became timid and retiring, sensitive to an excessive degree. One look was enough to reduce me to tears, and the only way I was content was to be left alone completely. I could not bear the company of strangers and found my joy only within the intimacy of the family" (S 34–35).

Thérèse had not worked through her grief regarding her mother's death at the time she entered boarding school, a situation that made her even more depressed. Thérèse exhibited the classical symptoms of depression—sad affect, low self-esteem, paralyzing indecisiveness, and the tendency to withdraw. Also, Thérèse's inability to tell her family about her pain compounded her depression for two reasons. First, what deepens depression is a feeling of helplessness, the sense that one is trapped in a situation with no way out. Thérèse was powerless to make friends at school; she didn't know how to defend herself, and she wasn't able to tell anyone, not even her second mother Pauline. "I didn't know how to defend myself and was content to cry without saying a word and without complaining *even to you* about what I was suffering" (S 53). Second, when a person cannot share pain, anxiety, or grief with the people she loves the most, that person's sense of isolation and loneliness is accentuated. And "the grief that does not speak whispers the o'erfraught heart and bids it to break" (*Macbeth* Act 4, Sc. 3). Thérèse was heading for a breakdown, and it was the loss of her second mother Pauline, who entered the convent *while* Thérèse was attending boarding school, that pushed her over the edge. But before we examine Thérèse's breakdown, let us consider the *good* that Thérèse was able to derive from her painful years at the boarding school.

A *Sensitive Heart*. Painful experiences like the one Thérèse had at the boarding school can make us bitter or can be the source of healing and growth, depending on how we relate to them. For several years I attended various ACOA (Adult Children of Alcoholics) meetings. I found one group to be very healing. After every meeting I went home feeling connected and normal. After attending another group, however, I often went away feeling either angry or full of self-pity. Both groups talked about the same issues and similar experiences, but what made the difference was *how* they talked about them. Those in the first group used insights about their painful past as a tool to deal with their dysfunctional behavior. In contrast, those in the second group seemed to be stuck in blame. Their recounting of the past was often nothing more than vitriolic diatribes that served no purpose other than to fester their wounds and provide justification for remaining angry and bitter.

Suffering is one of the great crossroads of life. It can transform or deform us. It can make us compassionate or self-centered. There is an old Native American proverb that says that the unwise person takes the manure of his life and out of the bitterness of his heart throws it at others, whereas the wise person gathers it to himself and uses it as fertilizer. If we are constantly chewing on the past like a dog gnawing on a bone, bitterness will poison our souls and infect our interpersonal relationships.

God taught Thérèse how to use the painful experiences of her life for good. "Jesus is teaching [Thérèse] to learn 'to draw profit from everything, *from the good* and *the bad* she finds in herself'" (L 795).[46] One example of how Thérèse drew profit from the bad in her life was how she related to what she felt about herself while she attended boarding school.

Alfred Adler writes that "children who have not been taught how to make contact with others feel alone when they enter school and as a result they are regarded as peculiar."[47] Such was the case with Thérèse. The other girls regarded her as somewhat strange because she didn't know how to play—even with dolls. In consequence, Thérèse wasn't a very pleasant companion, so she became an outsider who "walked sad and sick in the big yard" (S 87).

Thérèse's experience of being an outsider became a source of understanding and compassion. At community recreations, for example, Thérèse did not stay within the security of the familiar but reached out to those on the fringe of the group. "At recreation," testified Pauline, "she never went out of her way to meet her own three [blood] sisters. She chatted with any nun, no matter who she was, and especially with anyone she felt was lonely or left out."[48] How difficult is it when we are at a party or some gathering to leave the circle of one's friends and go over to the stranger standing in the corner and make small talk with him or her?

This was Thérèse's situation every day and it is also our own. We too live and work with people whom we don't like and who bore us to tears. But this situation is not an obstacle on the spiritual path because God does not ask us to *like* people but to *love* them. And in some mysterious way, the people we find most difficult to relate to are those whom God has brought into our lives for our sanctification. St. John of the Cross writes, "you should understand that those who are in the monastery are craftsmen placed there by God to mortify you by working and chiseling at you . . . so you become worthy of heaven" (Co 3).

John is presenting us with both a *reality* and a *choice*. The reality is that some people will grate on our nerves. The choice is whether we relate to them as *irritants* or agents of *transformation*. We may compare an irritating person to a grain of sand lodged in the tender membrane of an oyster. If we choose to bear this person's irritating mannerisms, foibles, and idiosyncrasies with love, then over time patience will produce a pearl. Thérèse made such a choice in the extreme during the last year of her life when she freely chose to work with Sister Marie of St. Joseph.

Sister Marie of St. Joseph was subject to severe mood swings. One moment she would be overly exuberant and in the next moment she would be in the depths of depression. Today, she would probably be diagnosed as being bipolar (manic-depressive). She was also subject to fits of violent outbursts of anger. Because of her unstable and volatile personality, all of the nuns kept their distance. In consequence, Sister Marie lived on the fringes of the community. She worked alone in the linen room because no one was willing to work with her. Over time, she became a very lonely and isolated human being. But there was a ray of hope for Sister Marie; her name was Thérèse.

Sister Marie went to the prioress and asked permission to receive guidance from Thérèse because she perceived in Thérèse both an understanding heart and a nonjudgmental mind. It is easy to imagine Thérèse identifying with the experience of Nick Carraway, the narrator of F. Scott Fitzgerald's novel *The Great Gatsby*. "I'm inclined to reserve all judgments, a habit that has opened up many curious natures to me. . . . The abnormal mind is quick to detect and attach itself to this quality in a normal person, and so . . . I was privy to the secret griefs of wild, unknown men."[49]

The secret griefs of Sister Marie became known to Thérèse, griefs with which Thérèse could identify. Like Thérèse, Sister Marie had lost her mother at a young age and knew the pain of being an outsider. Thérèse's own pain gave her the eyes to see Sister Marie in a way that no one else could. "If you knew her as well as I do," Thérèse said to Pauline, "you would see that she is not responsible for all of the things that seem so awful to us."[50] Thérèse tried to help Sister Marie but was under no illusions regarding what she could do for her. "She is to be pitied. She is like an old clock that has to be re-wound every quarter of an hour. Yes, it is as bad as that."[51] "If I had an infirmity such as hers, and so defective a spirit, I would not do any better than she does, and then I would despair."[52]

If you have ever had to minister to someone who was swallowed up in a black pit of depression and despair, then you know the utter helplessness and powerlessness that Thérèse must have felt in listening to Sister Marie. Thérèse knew that certain "infirmities [like Sister Marie's] are chronic, that there is no hope of a cure." But Thérèse also knew "that my mother would not cease to take care of me, to try to console me, if I remained sick all my life" (S 246). Thérèse listened to Sister Marie as a loving mother listens to her sick child, and it was out of the wisdom that flows from love that Thérèse ministered to her.

In the last year of her life, from March 1896 to May 1897, Thérèse volunteered to work with Sister Marie in the linen room. Commenting upon this time, Thérèse wrote, "This year . . . God has given me the grace to understand what charity is; I understood it before . . . but in an imperfect way. Ah! I understand now that charity consists in bearing with the faults of others, in not being surprised at their weakness, in being edified by the smallest acts of virtue we see them practice" (S 219–20). It is as if Thérèse is saying, "I thought I knew what being patient was all about, but after having worked in close quarters with Sister Marie, I realize that I didn't know the half of it. I found her presence difficult to bear, even oppressive at times. But as I gained understanding into the depths of her infirmity and how little she was capable of, I was truly edified by her smallest acts of virtue because I knew they took all of her strength. I believe that the best thing that I can do for her is to encourage her to focus on her gifts and talents, to help her to see the great significance of her life as a Carmelite, and to help draw her back into community life."

Thérèse encouraged Sister Marie in these areas, not merely by being a cheerleader, but in the Adlerian sense—by *giving courage* to another. Thérèse gave courage to Sister Marie by helping her to use her talents as a means of drawing her out of her isolation into the mainstream of the community. One way that Thérèse did this was by encouraging Sister Marie to use her beautiful singing voice to entertain the nuns at recreation. Another way was by means of imagery.

Thérèse used the image of a warrior to help Sister Marie change her behavior of fighting with the nuns to fighting her own demons. In two of her letters to Sister Marie, which dealt with a blow up between Sister Marie ("little brother") and one of the other nuns ("the first corporal"), Thérèse employed the imagery of combat to help Sister Marie re-image the *real* battle that she should be fighting—retaining patience instead of trying to win an argument. "I am not surprised at little brother's combats, but only that he loses his little bit of strength by surrendering his arms to the first corporal who is in his way" (L 1012). Thérèse is affirming the strength that she sees in Sister Marie.

This affirmation must have helped Sr. Marie tap into her ownstrength because the next letter that Thérèse wrote to her indicates that Sister Marie was successful in not "surrendering her arms." "All goes well. The little child is a brave one who deserves epaulettes of *gold*. . . . The rest goes well, too, since this little child . . . sleeps always on the Heart of the Great General. . . . Close to this Heart, we learn courage, and especially *confidence*. The hail of bullets, the noise of the cannon, what is all that when we are carried by the General?" (L 1013). There is a two-fold confidence that Thérèse is imparting to Sister Marie in this passage.

First, Thérèse is rejoicing with Sister Marie's accomplishment in controlling her temper. This may not sound like much, but think of a time in your life when you have struggled to overcome a fault in yourself to no avail. You're discouraged. And then one day, a friend of yours says to you, "You may not realize it, but your effort is very evident to everyone; keep up the good work." We know what happens as a result of this feedback. We feel energized and motivated to stay in the battle. This type of encouragement only takes a moment, but it can do so much for another person. The next time you *see* a person perform an act of kindness or even struggle to do so, *tell* the person about it. Perhaps one of the reasons we don't see more goodness in the world is that we don't say anything about the goodness that we do see. The first step in forming this habit is to *look for* goodness in others, instead of focusing on their faults and failings. This is what Thérèse did. "When I wish to increase this love in me, and when especially the devil tries to place before the eyes of my soul the faults of such and such a sister who is less attractive to me, I hasten to search out her virtues, her good intentions" (S 221). Seek and you will find. If we are looking for the mote in our brother's or sister's eye, we will find it, for none of us are perfect, but if we are searching out their virtues and good intentions, we will find them.

Second, Thérèse undergirded her encouraging feedback by telling Sister Marie that she didn't have to rely upon her own strength because she was "being carried by the General." Being carried by God is putting one's confidence in God's love and strength. It is not giving up the *effort* to change but rather giving up the *burden* of self-reliance, which is a source of discouragement. Putting one's confidence in God gives the soul encouragement because it is the "link between the soul's weakness and the strength it needs, the necessary bridge between humility and courage."[53]

Putting one's confidence in God's strength makes humility the foundation of courage. "It is beyond *my* strength," is transformed from an *excuse* for shrinking from the challenges of life into the *reason* why we can do all things, because we are relying upon God's strength rather than our own. "I saw immediately that the task was beyond my strength. I threw myself into the arms of God. . . . The moment I understood that it was impossible for me to do anything myself, the task you imposed upon me no longer appeared difficult. . . . If I had depended in the least on my own strength, I would very soon have had to give up" (S 238). Members of twelve-step programs know this paradox well. Admitting one's powerlessness, coming to believe that there is a power greater than oneself, and making a decision to hand over one's life to the care of God is not admitting defeat, but surrendering the illusion of self-sufficiency. Thérèse helped Sister Marie to put her hand in God's hand. This allowed her to be led.

Another way that Thérèse encouraged Sister Marie was to help her to see the significance and meaning of her life, to help her grasp that her daily struggles and acts of love had eternal value because they helped in the work of the salvation of souls. Thérèse did this by tapping into something they shared—zeal for the missions. In one of her letters to Sister Marie, Thérèse wrote, "Ah! how beautiful is the little child's vocation! It is not *one mission* that she must evangelize but *all missions*. How will she do this? . . . By *loving* . . . by THROWING FLOWERS to Jesus . . . [who] will take these flowers, and, giving them an inestimable value, He will throw them in His turn; He will have them fly over all shores and will save souls with the flowers, with *the love of the little child,* who will see nothing but will always smile even through her tears" (L 989–90).

The older we become, the more we question the significance of our lives. As we are gradually stripped of all that we have based our personal significance upon—youth, beauty, strength, accomplishments, reputation, and power—their influence begins to fade. When we are no longer able to do the work by which we have defined ourselves, and when we can't even maintain the illusionary dreams that we have for our children because they are no longer children, we begin to be haunted by questions regarding the significance and meaning of our lives. With most of our life behind us, we begin to question its value. "Will it have made any difference that I was born? Will the world be a better place because I have passed through it?"

By her letter, Thérèse grounded Sister Marie in what constituted the true significance of her life—what *God* was doing through her *in her struggles,* "through her tears," as Thérèse put it. Thérèse was telling Sister Marie that her life, *as it was,* right in the midst of her emotional problems and isolation, had "inestimable value" because God was using her acts of love to save souls.

There is a voice within the innermost depths of our souls that instinctively tells us that if our life is to have any real meaning at all, then it must be connected to that which will last forever. As immortal creatures made in God's image and likeness, we can only be energized by the conviction that our life's project is making a contribution to that which is Eternal. Teilhard de Chardin wrote:

> The more I examine myself, the more I discover this psychological truth: that no one lifts his little finger to do the smallest task unless moved, however obscurely, by the conviction that he is contributing infinitesimally (at least indirectly) to the building of something definitive—that is to say, to your work, my God. This may sound strange or exaggerated to those who act without thoroughly scrutinizing themselves. And yet it is a fundamental law of their action. It requires no less than the pull of what men call the Absolute, no less than you yourself, to set in motion the frail liberty which you have given us. And that being so, everything which diminishes my explicit faith in the heavenly value of the results of my endeavor, diminishes irremediably my power to act.[54]

Thérèse helped Sister Marie believe that her actions had heavenly value, an "inestimable value," because they contributed to something eternal, the salvation of souls. By engendering this conviction in Sister Marie, Thérèse helped to draw her out of her isolation and loneliness by making her aware that her life participated in an enterprise greater than herself—the kingdom of God. Vision is what Thérèse engendered in Sister Marie, a vision of her life as a small but significant part of the great spiritual adventure of humankind, a vision that functioned as a safeguard and counterweight to the centripetal force of her tendency toward self-absorption.

But as important as it is to have confidence in the power of God and to see the true significance of one's life, it is far more important to believe that we are loved as we are—warts and all. Considering that most of the members of Lisieux Carmel avoided Sister Marie as much as possible, how difficult must it have been for her to believe in God's unconditional love? Thérèse knew this, and, in consequence, wrote a poem for Sister Marie (*The Eternal Canticle Sung Even in Exile*) that emphasized that God loved her as she was. The refrain of the poem is as follows: "Forgetting my great misery / You come to dwell in my heart / My weak Love, ah, what a mystery! / Is enough to captivate you Lord" (PT 142). To hear these words as Sister Marie must have heard them, we must situate ourselves within the relationship that developed between Thérèse and Sister Marie during the year that they worked together in the linen room.

We all know from experience that *who* is speaking to us will determine the impact of *what* is being spoken. For example, if a person you deeply respect and admire says, "I'm very proud of you," these words will mean infinitely more to you than if they were spoken by someone whom you do not hold in high regard. Similarly, our hearts can only be touched by the words, "God loves you," when they are spoken by a person whom we know loves us deeply, who knows everything about us, the good and the bad, and loves us all the more. This was the situation that existed between Thérèse and Sister Marie.

Thérèse knew it all. She knew Sister Marie's childhood history, the depths of her brokenness, her self-hate, and the fierce battle that she waged against her moods. It was out of this knowledge that Thérèse was able to communicate to Sister Marie the love and mercy of God. For many of us, there is a conflict between God's mercy and justice. This was not true for Thérèse. In fact, she believed that God is merciful *because* God is just. God is so just that, when he judges us, he takes into consideration everything about us, and as a result is merciful. "To me He has granted His *infinite Mercy* and *through it* I contemplate and adore the other divine perfections! All of these perfections appear to be resplendent *with love*; even His Justice (and perhaps this even more so than the others) seems to me clothed in *love*. What a sweet joy it is to think that God is *just*, i.e., that He takes into account our weakness, that He is perfectly aware of our fragile nature" (S 180). Thérèse was a sacrament of God's loving mercy for Sister Marie, who communicated to her the infinite mercy of God who takes into account the weaknesses of our frail human nature. Thérèse's loving presence touched Sister Marie deeply and continued to do so long after Thérèse died in 1897.

In 1909, because her mental condition had so deteriorated, Sister Marie left Lisieux Carmel at the age of fifty-five, after spending twenty-eight years in religious life. She died in 1936 at the age of seventy-eight after many years of wandering aimlessly about the French countryside. However, she kept in touch with Lisieux Carmel. In 1929, she wrote the following to Pauline (Mother Agnes). "The work of sanctification which my beloved Thérèse began so lovingly in me before she died still continues. And I can say in all sincerity that—my house is at rest. And I live now in complete abandonment. As long as I love Jesus, and He and Thérèse are pleased, nothing else matters to me."[55]

When Sister Marie left Carmel, there was something that she did not leave behind—the poem that Thérèse had written for her. In the years that followed her departure, the word *exile* proved to have symbolic significance far beyond what Thérèse had ever intended. I like to think that in her wanderings, the poem was like manna in the desert, that it was one of the means through which Thérèse's love continued to be her daily bread. But beyond the sacrament of the poem, Thérèse's interceding presence continued to support Sister Marie.

When Thérèse was fourteen, she prayed for the soul of the convicted murderer Pranzini, whom she called her "first child," and prayed for him until the day that she died. Once, when Thérèse was having a Mass said for Pranzini, she said to Céline, "It's for my child. . . . I mustn't abandon him now."[56] Thérèse, who had said that she would spend her time in heaven doing good on earth, certainly did not abandon her "child" Sister Marie. As Sister Marie wandered around France, she did not wander alone. She had a companion at her side, someone who loved her, someone who truly understood her loneliness, the presence of a saint who once had been a frightened, lonely little girl who "walked sad and sick in the big yard" (S 87).

The Gathering Storm

THÉRÈSE SURVIVED HER FIRST YEAR (1881–1882) at boarding school. She was looking forward to spending a happy summer with her family at Les Buissonnets, only to be overwhelmed with one of the most devastating blows that she would ever receive in her life, the news that her "second mother" Pauline would be leaving home to enter the Carmelite convent in Lisieux. To understand the magnitude of this event, we need to interpret it within the context of Thérèse's life, her early separation experiences from mother figures, the death of Zélie, and how these events impacted Thérèse's psyche, namely, that she began to cling to her family. Thus, it would have been traumatic for Thérèse if *any* member of her family was to leave home, but this was especially true regarding Pauline. In order to understand why this is true, we must first explore the depth of the emotional bond that existed between Thérèse and Pauline.

Thérèse's Relationship to Pauline. On the day of Zélie's funeral, Pauline (age sixteen) became Thérèse's (age four and a half) "second mother." Thérèse writes:

> The day the Church blessed the mortal remains of our dear mother, now in heaven, God willed to give me another mother on earth. He willed also that I choose her freely. All five of us were gathered together, looking at each other sadly. Louise was there too, and, seeing Céline and me, she said: "Poor little things, you have no mother any more!" Céline threw her arms around Marie saying: "Well, you will be my Mama."

> Accustomed to following Céline's example, I turned instead to you, Mother . . . I threw myself into your arms, crying: "Well, as for me, it's Pauline who will be my Mama!" (S 34)

It is impossible to exaggerate the influence that Pauline had on Thérèse. It may be argued that all the influence was not good; nevertheless, the impact was enormous. First, Pauline performed all the daily motherly tasks for Thérèse—waking her up, helping her to say her prayers, dressing her, combing her hair, making her breakfast. "In the morning you used to come to me and ask me if I had raised my heart to God, and then you dressed me. While dressing me you spoke about Him and afterward we knelt down and said our prayers together. The reading lesson came later" (S 36). These two sentences speak of daily routines and rituals of great intimacy that we should not pass over quickly. Let us briefly explore the full import of what is contained in the simple phrase, "While dressing me you spoke. . . ."

For all of us, there are points of contact built into the circumstances of our lives that afford opportunities for interpersonal exchange. For example, when I was growing up, my brother Frank and I shared the same bedroom. We would often talk before falling asleep. Our conversations sometimes revolved around what had gone on in school, who would win the World Series, and so forth. At other times, we thought up new and creative ways of how we and our friend Bill could terrorize the neighborhood. But sometimes our conversations drifted into very personal matters. We talked, for example, about the impact that our father's drinking was having upon our home or what we wanted to do when we grew up.

This is the way it is with someone to whom you are bonded. You begin to chat about the movie that is playing at the Rialto and, before you know it, a stream of associations has gradually steered the conversation into deep waters. This is how it must have been between Thérèse and Pauline.

> *Pauline:* Thérèse, would you like to wear your blue dress today?
>
> *Thérèse:* Oh! Yes. It's my favorite. Pauline: It's also Papa's favorite.
>
> *Thérèse:* Pauline, yesterday when Papa was up on the ladder, he said, "Move away, little one, if I fall, I'll crush you!" Pauline, I was afraid. I'm not "able to think of Papa *dying* without trembling" (cf. S 47).
>
> *Pauline:* O Thérèse, you're trembling now. Come here, let me hold you.
>
> *Thérèse:* Pauline, will Papa die, like Mama? I don't know if I can. . . .

Even though we do not know exactly what transpired between Thérèse and Pauline during these morning rituals or how they had an impact on Thérèse, we do know this much. The words and deeds of those whom we hold in high regard, whom we respect, or whose opinions we value, impact our lives greatly and mean more to us than the approval of a multitude.

In Peter Shaffer's play *Amadeus,* when Salieri finally obtained the fame that he had always longed for, he knew that it was absolutely worthless because his music was applauded by those ignorant of its worth. "I was bricked up in fame! Embalmed in fame! Buried in fame. . . . This was my sentence: I must endure thirty years of being called 'Distinguished' by people incapable of distinguishing!" By contrast, how much more would it have meant to Salieri, if Mozart, whom he considered "[God's] Incarnation," had said *one word* of praise to him regarding his music?[57]

It is not just *what* is said to us that makes a difference, but *who* says it. The words that Pauline spoke to Thérèse carried great weight because of the mother-daughter bond that existed between them. At Les Buissonnets, Pauline had become the central authority figure in Thérèse's life.

> Papa himself was obliged to conform to your will, without *Pauline's* consent I didn't even take a walk, and when Papa told me to come I'd answer: "*Pauline* doesn't want it." Then he'd come and ask your permission and to please him, Pauline would say "Yes," but little Thérèse saw by her look that she wasn't saying it with all her heart, and she'd begin to cry and would not be consoled until Pauline said "Yes" and *kissed her with all her heart!* (S 44)

The important thing to notice in this passage is that Thérèse was highly attuned to Pauline's facial expressions and the tone of her voice. Thérèse was able to perceive the slightest incongruence between Pauline's words and their underlying meaning: "Thérèse saw by her look that she wasn't saying it with all her heart" (S 44).

The more that children need their parents' approval or are afraid of being abandoned by them, the more highly developed is their radar. This is because their emotional survival depends upon their ability to perceive and accurately interpret the meaning of their parents' every word, gesture, and tone of voice. It is also worth noting in the above passage that, even *before* her father came to take her out for a walk, Thérèse already *knew* what Pauline was feeling. "When Papa told me to come I'd answer: '*Pauline* doesn't want it'" (S 44). And even when Pauline *said* yes, Thérèse knew that she didn't say it wholeheartedly.

As the above passage indicates, the maternal bond that existed between Pauline and Thérèse was strong *after* Zélie's death, but it was also strong *before* she died. From a psychological perspective,

Pauline was not only Thérèse's "second mother;" she was also her "first mother." Let us look at the evidence to substantiate this claim from the framework of psychologist Heinz Kohut.

Mirroring. Kohut writes that the *sine qua non* for healthy human development is positive *mirroring.* Positive mirroring happens when another human being takes delight in our accomplishments and empathizes with our pain. In the process, our self-image is "mirrored" back to us. In short, when we experience that we are the apple of someone's eye, we feel valued, loved, and significant.

We all need positive mirroring throughout life, but for a small child, whose self-image is being formed, positive mirroring is crucial for healthy psychological growth. Without it, the child's self-esteem becomes fragile and she is vulnerable to self-doubt. In short, a child feels insecure because she questions whether or not she is loved.

The primary mirror for a child is her mother. And considering Zélie's depressive personality, her mental absorption in the deaths of four of her children (esp. Hélène, of whom Zélie said, "There is not a moment of the day when I am not thinking of her" [S 3]), her preoccupation with her lace business, her anxiety about her children (esp. Léonie), her breast cancer and its concomitant fear of death, it is reasonable to ask the question: did Zélie have the capacity to function as an adequate mirror for Thérèse? Let us explore one of Thérèse's earliest memories in regard to this question.

When Thérèse was two years old she accompanied her mother on a train trip to Le Mans to visit Zélie's sister, Sister Marie-Dosithée (Marie-Louise Guérin). Sister Marie gave Thérèse a basket of candy to bring back home. The basket contained two sugar rings that made Thérèse exclaim, "How wonderful! there will be a ring for Céline also!" (S 23). Unfortunately, one of the rings fell out of the basket. "I had nothing now to give Céline and so was filled with grief! I asked if I could retrace my steps, but Mama seemed to pay no attention to me. This was too much and my *tears* were followed by loud *cries*. I was unable to understand why she didn't share my pain, and this only increased my grief" (S 23).

This passage is of special significance because it is not taken from one of Zélie's letters as are so many of the events that are recorded about Thérèse's childhood in the early chapters of *Story of a Soul*. Rather, it is one of Thérèse's earliest memories about her relationship with her mother. Granted, this memory tells us more about Thérèse than it does about Zélie; nevertheless, does it not also indicate Zélie's inability to be empathically present to Thérèse?[58] Psychologist Robert J. Giugliano, commenting upon this passage writes:

> The above memory is not only of a particular event but also one that represents a pattern in Zélie and Thérèse's relationship. Zélie was not able to respond to or emotionally connect with Thérèse when Thérèse was emotionally distressed and in need of calming and soothing attention. This pattern of relationship is typical of mothers and infants who are insecurely attached. . . . Zélie apparently was not emotionally available to Thérèse during the beginning of the trip when Thérèse remembers crying but doesn't understand why. . . . Thérèse experienced her mother's emotional absence and failure to respond to her feelings and she wonders why her mother was not able to share her pain.[59]

Giugliano's statement is not a judgment upon Zélie as a loving mother but an observation regarding her inability to be emotionally present to Thérèse. We will never know the exact nature of the emotional bond that existed between Zélie and Thérèse. But if, for the sake of argument, we presuppose that Zélie was not able to provide adequate mirroring for Thérèse, then Thérèse may have instinctively tried to bond with Pauline "as mother" before Zélie died. So what happens when a mother's mirroring is either faulty or inadequate?

Idealizing. Kohut says that the child has two chances at emotional health as her identity is being formed. If she is not able to receive adequate mirroring from her mother, then she will compensate for this lack by finding someone she can *idealize*. This is not to say that the need for *idealizing* is an auxiliary need that emerges *only* when the need for *mirroring* is not met. However, when *mirroring* is inadequate, a child will seek to be connected to an admired and respected (idealized) person. This is because being connected to an idealized adult (someone who is regarded as being all powerful, wise, and good) makes a child feel secure and significant (*idealizing needs*).[60]

Long before Zélie died, Pauline was the idealized figure in Thérèse's life. One of Thérèse's earliest memories (age 2) is the following:

> I was very proud of my two [older] sisters, but the one who was my *ideal* from childhood was Pauline. When I was beginning to talk, Mama would ask me: "What are you thinking about?" and I would answer invariably: "Pauline!" Another time, I was moving my little finger over the windowpanes and I said: "I'm writing Pauline!" . . . You were my *ideal;* I wanted to be like you." (S 20)

Pauline as an idealized person was the stable, calming presence for Thérèse at Alençon, a presence that Zélie could not provide. In this sense, Pauline was Thérèse's "first mother." It is within this perspective that we can begin to understand why Pauline's entrance into Carmel was so traumatic for Thérèse.

Just as a truck breaks down if there is either a structural weakness in its undercarriage or if it is carrying an excessive load, so too Thérèse was vulnerable to a breakdown. The undercarriage of her psyche was weak because of her history of early separations from mother figures. Also, she was carrying an enormous load of stress as the result of attending boarding school. Thérèse was at the breaking point when Pauline left home and entered Carmel. Let us now explore the factors that triggered Thérèse's illness.

But You Promised

"Life is made of ever so many partings welded together."[61] From the moment we are born we begin to mourn; we mourn the security of the womb, the wonder of childhood, and the halcyon days of youth. We mourn our classmates whom we have outgrown or who have outgrown us. We mourn friends who have moved away, left us behind, or have died. We pine away over unrequited love, outworn romantic dreams, and the prince charming who never came. We grieve over the unrealistic aspirations and ambitions that never came to be and the illusionary dreams that we have for our children. We must mourn the things that never were and never will be, and all things that the coming of age and the inroads of time wrest away from us—our youth, our strength, our beauty, our loved ones, our memory, our health, and life itself.

Thérèse came to realize at a very tender age the hard fact that we must endure loss at every stage of life's journey. When she found out that Pauline was going to enter the convent and leave her behind, she awoke to the painful realization that life is made up of ever so many partings welded together. "In one instant, I understood what life was; until then, I had never seen it so sad; but it appeared to me in all its reality, and I saw it was nothing but a continual suffering and separation" (S 58).

Because all partings are welded together, we revisit and rework the separations of the past in the separations of the present. Because Thérèse's separation from Pauline was welded to the death of her mother, Thérèse would have to return to her mother's deathbed and mourn anew. But what made the loss of Pauline different from the loss of Zélie was that there was an element of betrayal attached to it.

> I had said to Pauline, one day, that I would like to be a hermit and go away with her alone in a faraway desert place. She answered that my desire was also hers and that she *was waiting* for me to be big enough for her to leave. This was no doubt not said seriously, but little Thérèse had taken it seriously; and how she suffered when she heard her dear Pauline speaking one day to Marie about her coming entrance into Carmel. I didn't know what Carmel was, but I understood that Pauline was going to leave me to enter a convent. I understood too, she *would not wait for me* and I was about to lose my second *mother!* Ah! how can I express the anguish of my heart! (S 57–58)

In order to understand Thérèse's anguish we must enter into the mind of a child.

Egocentrism. Because children view the universe only from the perspective of their needs and feelings, they do not have the capacity to see things objectively. For example, if you tell a child that you will take her to the zoo on Saturday, but have to break your promise because Friday night your boss said that you had to come into work the following day, the child doesn't have the capacity to understand why you can't take her. It is completely beyond the child's capacity to comprehend how *anything* can take precedence over taking her to the zoo. "But you promised!" is an expression of unbelief.

As adults, we can become angry or disappointed when a person either reneges on a promise or is unable to fulfill it, but we have the capacity to understand that the fulfillment of a promise is contingent upon numerous factors. For example, if one of my community members promises that he will help me to paint the stairway in the monastery on Saturday, but he comes down with the flu on Friday night, "Well that's life!" Such a perspective is outside the realm of a child. Thérèse was only nine years old when she discovered that Pauline was going to enter a convent. Because of her tender age and her deep anxiety surrounding parental abandonment, Thérèse did not have the capacity to understand how Pauline could make a life choice independent of how it would affect her. For this nine-year-old child who was frightened to death of being abandoned, Pauline was not going to enter the convent; rather she "was going to *leave me*" (S 58, emphasis added). For Thérèse, Pauline was not an adult going ahead with her life; rather she was her second mother who "*would not wait for me*" (S 58).

Innocence and Trust. Children look upon adults they idealize as gods in whom they place an absolute trust. Like God, if they *say* something is true, then it *is* true. "And God *said* let there be . . . and so it *was*." "But you *said* so! But you *promised!*" All parents know the disbelief, confusion, and rage contained in these words as they are said by their child in the face of a broken promise. Underlying all these emotions is fear. For a broken promise undermines a child's sense of security and predictability; "Because mommy and daddy are all knowing and all good, I can count on the world *being* what they say it *is*."

Promises also give children hope in times of stress. Promises assure them that even though the present is fearful, ultimately everything will be all right. This is why most children prefer traditional fairytales to modern ones. "When children are asked to name their favorite fairy tales, hardly any modern tales are among their choices . . . [because they] fail to provide the escape and consolation which the fearsome events in the [traditional] fairy tale make necessary, to strengthen the child for meeting the vagaries of his life. Without such encouraging conclusions, the child, after listening to the story, would feel that there is indeed no hope of extricating himself from the despairs of his life."[62] A promise made to a child from an idealized adult functions like a traditional fairy tale; it provides hope of being extricated from a despairing situation. Such was the case with Thérèse.

Thérèse was in a despairing situation. She was going through "the saddest [time] of [her] life" (S 53) when Pauline broke her promise that one day she would "go away with her alone in a faraway desert place . . . and that she *was waiting* for [Thérèse] to be big enough for her to leave" (S 57). This was a promise that Thérèse "had taken . . . seriously" (S 58) and *had* to take seriously, for it gave Thérèse both the assurance that there was light at the end of the tunnel and the strength to endure the journey through the darkness.

The assurance that Thérèse was given by Pauline was the deepest assurance that anyone could receive from another human being. Not only was it given by the person she trusted most, but the promise was an expression of *desire* on Pauline's part (at least this is how Thérèse must have understood Pauline's words). When Thérèse confided to Pauline, "I would like to . . . go away with [you] alone in a faraway desert place . . . [Pauline] answered that *my* desire was also *hers*" (S 57, emphases added).

Reflect upon your own life for a moment. Don't you feel that it is less likely that your spouse or a friend will walk out of your life if you know that he or she *wants* to be with you? Don't you feel more loved and secure in a relationship when the other person *desires* to be with you as much as you desire to be with him or her?

Graham Greene once said that we never get accustomed to being less important to people than they are to us. And what we can never get accustomed to in an unequal relationship is the insecurity that the inequality of desire engenders within us. For we instinctively know that desire is the bond that keeps a person from leaving us. Therefore, when Pauline told Thérèse that she shared her desire to go away together to a faraway place, Pauline gave Thérèse a deep sense of security that she would never leave her. This was shattered. And the crowning blow was *how* Thérèse received the devastating news. She overheard it in a conversation that Pauline was having with Marie.

"If I had learned of my dear Pauline's departure very gently, I would not have suffered as much perhaps, but having heard about it by surprise, it was as if a sword were buried in my heart" (S 58). This was a deep wound for two reasons. First, it was a breach of intimacy. Think of a time when you heard news *secondhand* about an important decision that a dear friend had made in his or her life. How did you feel? Second, the news was a deep psychic jolt because it caught Thérèse off guard; she did not have the time to absorb the shock. Psychologist Fritz Kunkel writes that if a "Breach-of-the-We [that is, a feeling of unity between a child and parent] occurs quickly . . . [and] suddenly . . . it generates a terrifying feeling of fear, helplessness, and estrangement. Beyond doubt this is the most terrifying experience of childhood."[63]

As adults, we all know the numbing shock and terrifying feeling of being trapped in a sense of unreality at the sudden news of the death of a loved one. And if the shock is more than we can bear, then in order to survive, we need to deny reality and cling to every hope, no matter how false.

In F. Scott Fitzgerald's short story, *The Long Way Out,* Mrs. King, who has just been discharged from a mental ward, is waiting in the lobby of the hospital for her husband to come and take her home. Tragically, he is killed in an auto accident en route. The staff feels that Mrs. King cannot bear up under the weight of the news of her husband's death. Therefore, they tell her that he called to say that he has been detained at the office and that he will pick her up the following day. Mrs. King was disappointed but said, "After all these months what's one more day?" So, every day for years Mrs. King got dressed and took her suitcase to the lobby to wait for her husband to come, only to be told that he was delayed, and that he would come tomorrow.

"'We tried to tell her,' Dr. Pirie said. 'She laughed and said we were trying to see if she was still sick. You could use the word unthinkable in an exact sense here—his death is unthinkable to her.'"[64] Pauline's departure was an unthinkable death for Thérèse; it was a loss that was too heavy for her to bear. And under its weight—she collapsed.

Pauline Is Lost to Me

ON THE MORNING OF OCTOBER 2, 1882, Thérèse returned to the boarding school and Pauline left home—never to return. That afternoon, when Thérèse visited Pauline, her unthinkable fear began to surface.

> In the afternoon, Aunt came to get us to go to Carmel and I saw *my Pauline* behind the *grille*. Ah! how I suffered from this *visit* to Carmel! . . . The sufferings which preceded your entrance were nothing in comparison with those which followed it. Every Thursday we went *as a family* to Carmel and I, accustomed to talk heart to heart with *Pauline,* obtained with great trouble two or three minutes at the end of the visit. It is understood, of course, that I spent them in crying and left with a broken heart. I didn't understand that it was through consideration for Aunt that you were directing your words to Jeanne and Marie instead of speaking to your little girls. I didn't understand and I said in the depths of my heart: "Pauline is lost to me!" It is surprising to see how much my mind developed in the midst of suffering; it developed to such a degree that it wasn't long before I became sick. (S 59–60)

This passage records three layers of the loss of intimacy that Thérèse experienced when Pauline entered Carmel: the loss of a *quality* or *dimension* of intimacy; the loss of *opportunities* to be intimate; and what Thérèse perceived to be the *death* of her relationship with Pauline.

The Loss of a Dimension of Intimacy. If we hope to understand what Thérèse suffered when Pauline entered Carmel, we need to pay attention to the words that she emphasizes in the text. "I saw *my Pauline* behind the *grille*" (S 59). This is not a *statement* but a *gasp*, an expression of shock, fear, and bewilderment. Pauline was present but not fully accessible, for the grille had severed a very important dimension of their relationship—tactility.

We may naively think that the grille only involved a *physical* separation, but in human intercourse, we are impacted both psychologically and emotionally, when the immediacy of physical contact with a loved one is either severed or restricted. For example, we all know the difference between talking to a dear friend over the phone and in person. Over the phone, our friend is *present* but he or she is also *absent*. Who hasn't felt lonely *while* speaking to a loved one over the phone? We all know the truth of Charles Dickens's statement that electronic communication will never be a substitute for the human face.[65]

Similarly, *seeing* Pauline behind the grille could never be a substitute for *touching* and *being held* by her. The grille had amputated a vital dimension of Thérèse's relationship with Pauline. For Thérèse, the experience of speaking to Pauline through the grille must have been similar to speaking to a loved one over the phone; Pauline was present but also absent. One can imagine Thérèse saying to herself, "I *saw* my Pauline behind the grille, my Pauline, who tucked me into bed and kissed me goodnight, who dressed me, combed my hair, whose lap I often curled up on, and who held me close to her when I was afraid. How was I going *to be* with her, now that I can't touch her? I don't know any other way to relate to her."

Within the space of a few hours, Thérèse was faced with an enormous task of adjustment for which she was ill prepared. In the morning, "I received *Pauline's* last kiss," and in the afternoon, "I saw *my Pauline* behind the *grille*" (S 59). How was this nine-year-old child going to find a new way to relate to the most important person in her life?

The Loss of Opportunities to be Intimate. "Ah! how I suffered from this *visit* to Carmel! . . . Every Thursday we went *as a family* to Carmel and I, accustomed to talk heart to heart with *Pauline,* obtained with great trouble two or three minutes at the end of the visit" (S 60). Thérèse was starving to talk heart to heart with *her Pauline,* but the presence of her *family* made a *real visit* impossible. We all know Thérèse's situation. We cannot talk freely to a loved one when the presence of another person renders impossible the exchange of intimacies.

To be deprived of intimate conversation with the person you are accustomed to talking heart to heart with on one given day is frustrating, but to be deprived of such conversation over a long period of time is a great loss that engenders deep loneliness. For when we cannot express what is in our hearts and receive the great gift of being truly heard and understood, we feel isolated and imprisoned within ourselves with all our pent-up emotions and unexpressed thoughts. Carl Rogers, reflecting upon his experience as a psychotherapist, writes:

> I have often noticed that the more deeply I hear the meanings of this person, the more there is that happens. Almost always, when a person realizes he has been deeply heard, his eyes moisten. I think in some real sense he is weeping for joy. It is as though he were saying, "Thank God, somebody heard me. Someone knows what it's like to be me." In such moments I have had the fantasy of a prisoner in a dungeon, tapping out day after day a Morse code message, "Does anybody hear me? Is anybody there?" And finally one day

he hears some faint tappings which spell out "Yes." By that one simple response he is released from his loneliness; he has become a human being again.⁶⁶

As Thérèse sat in the corner of the speak room and whimpered, she was tapping out a message to Pauline. "Pauline, can't you see how much I miss you? Can't you understand how much I need to talk to you *alone*? Please, talk to me, notice me!" But Thérèse's efforts fell upon deaf ears. "We hardly paid any attention to her childish prattle" (L 151).

The Death of a Relationship. This experience of being ignored was the basis of Thérèse's belief that a radical change had taken place in Pauline's relationship toward her, so radical that Thérèse felt that she had *lost* Pauline. "I didn't understand that it was through consideration for Aunt that you were directing your words to Jeanne and Marie instead of speaking to your little girls. I didn't understand and I said in the depths of my heart: 'Pauline is lost to me!'" (S 60). This may seem to be an extreme interpretation that Thérèse projected upon Pauline's behavior. However, we must try to see it through the lens of Thérèse's history of separations from mother figures that seared her psyche with the belief that all human bonds, even the deepest bonds, are fragile and unstable. What else could Thérèse conclude? That morning Pauline had warmly kissed her good-bye; a few hours later, it was as if she didn't exist.

Think of it for a moment. When you are in pain because a person you deeply love has moved away, what makes the pain bearable is the knowledge that your loved one feels the same pain. His or her pain is the assurance that you are still loved. But what happens when, over a period of time, the relationship becomes a one-way street? What happens when you are the only one who is taking initiatives to keep in touch? What happens when you never forget to send a birthday card, a Christmas card, a Valentine card, etc., but more often than not, you never receive one in return? What happens when you call your friend on the phone and he or she is the one who always ends the conversation? "It was good talking to you, but there is some work I need to get done before I go to bed tonight. Take care. I'll call you next week." But you know that he or she never will. So, what do you do? Do you continue to try to keep up the relationship? Or do you allow it to die a natural death? Do you continue to pretend that there is something between you and the other person? Or do you admit the hard truth that it is all over? If we as adults find such a death so hard to bear, how much more painful would it be for a nine-year-old child who believes that the most important person in her life no longer loves her?

Stress Begins to Take its Toll. Thérèse kept everything bottled up inside of herself. But as she "walked sad and sick in the big yard" (S 87), her burden began to manifest itself in the form of headaches. "It started with violent headaches," testified Léonie, "and [Thérèse] began to have these almost immediately after Pauline entered Carmel."[67] And by "the end of the year, I began to have a constant headache" (S 60). But because "I was able to pursue my studies . . . nobody was worried about me" (S 60).

No one worried about Thérèse because no one suspected that anything was wrong. She was very good at masking her feelings. It was a habit ingrained from childhood. For example, regarding the death of her mother, Thérèse wrote that she did not "speak to anyone about the feelings I experienced . . . [and] no one had any time to pay attention to me" (S 33). Now again, Thérèse could not tell anyone *directly* how much she was suffering, so she began to tap out a distress call, hoping that someone would hear her call for help. At first, the call was merely whimpering in the corner of the speak room, but when no one paid any attention to her childish prattle, she had to shout for her family to notice her pain. "It wasn't long before I became sick" (S 60).

A Sorrow too Deep for Tears

THÉRÈSE'S HEADACHES PERSISTED throughout the following spring as she continued to attend boarding school and mourn the loss of Pauline. Around Christmas, other disturbing symptoms began to appear. Thérèse started having pains in her stomach and side, developed a rash, lost her appetite, and suffered from insomnia. "Nobody [had been] worried about me" (S 60), writes Thérèse, but her symptoms began to speak so loudly that her family began to be concerned. Pauline wrote the following to Thérèse toward the end of December 1882: "Your poor little Pauline . . . is dreaming at night about the pains in your side, your head, your heart, your pimples, and your ointments" (L 154). And again: "My poor little patient, How are you today? Has your headache eased up a little? Say 'yes,' I beg you. Dear baby, don't be sick anymore like that. Don't you know you are distressing me, that you are causing me worries. And worry is such an ugly flower! Little one, you would be more lovable by showing me some beautiful roses on your face, always so pale" (L 156–57).

Pauline's concern reassured Thérèse that she was still loved, that Pauline was *not* lost to her. Nevertheless, the letters could not give Thérèse the only thing she *really* wanted—Pauline herself. The letters were only palliative; they were not curative. They could not heal Thérèse's fragile psyche; they could only relieve her pain temporarily. But during Lent, even this relief was unavailable to her, for Lisieux Carmel forbade any correspondence or visits during the Church's penitential season. Thérèse reached her breaking point toward the end of Lent when her father took Léonie and Marie to Paris and left Thérèse and Céline behind with the Guérins. This separation was too much for Thérèse to bear. She began to experience separation anxiety and started to call her Aunt Céline "Mama." Whereupon, her cousin said to Thérèse, "She's my Mama, she's not yours. Your Mama is dead."

Then, "One evening Uncle took me for a walk and spoke about Mama and about past memories with a kindness that touched me profoundly and made me cry. . . . That night we were to go to the Catholic Circle meeting, but finding I was too fatigued, Aunt made me go to bed; when I was undressing, I was seized with a strange trembling. Believing I was cold, Aunt covered me with blankets and surrounded me with hot water bottles. But nothing was able to stop my shaking, which lasted almost all night. . . . [Uncle] went to get Doctor Notta the next day, and he judged . . . that I had a very serious illness and one which had never before attacked a child as young as I" (S 60–61).

Dr. Notta's official diagnosis was chorea (St. Vitus's dance) because Thérèse's symptoms were very similar to those of chorea (headaches, attacks of shivering, violent contortions of the body, anxiety, hallucinations). Yet, there was *something* about Thérèse's case that made Dr. Notta doubt his own diagnosis. He thought that Thérèse's illness was hysteria but dismissed his intuition because of Thérèse's age. He said to Isidore Guérin, "In a fourteen- or fifteen-year-old such a phenomenon might be easily explained, but never in a child of eleven."[68]

The reason Notta dismissed his intuition was because, in his day, hysteria was thought to emerge only after the onset of puberty. And since Thérèse had not reached the age of puberty, Notta discounted hysteria as a possible diagnosis. However, looking back over the span of a hundred years, we should not discard Dr. Notta's intuition too hastily. Rather, let us explore his hunch, for it may shed light on Thérèse's illness.

Studies in Hysteria. In mid-October 1885, two men boarded trains in Eastern Europe bound for Paris. The first was Thérèse's father, who was returning home from making a pilgrimage in Eastern Europe. The second was an obscure Viennese doctor named Sigmund Freud, who would spend the next five months in the City of Lights studying the etiology of hysteria with the eminent French physician Jean Martin Charcot. Perhaps Louis and Sigmund crossed one another's path.

Freud's work with Charcot helped to confirm his own thinking on hysteria. He published his findings in his seminal work, *Studies in Hysteria* (1895), written in collaboration with Josef Breuer. This early work contains the seeds of both Freud's most important discovery and his most erroneous conclusion about the nature of neurotic conflicts.

At this early date in his career, Freud did not attribute *all* neuroses to repressed sexuality, but said that a "great majority" of neuroses were sexual in their etiology.[69] Over time, Freud generalized from his culture-bound clinical practice and eventually erred when he stated that *all* neurotic conflicts are sexual in nature. Erich Fromm writes that Freud's clients "were repressed in the society in which Freud lived—more specifically, in the middle class, with its Victorian morality, from which Freud and most of his patients came. What he did was to identify the social structure of his class and its problems with the problems inherent in human existence. This was one of Freud's blind spots."[70] It is rare for a psychologist of our day to encounter the same type of client that Freud did in his.[71]

Freud's over-sexualization of his theory of neurosis is very unfortunate. For it has overshadowed his earlier findings that "any experience which calls up distressing affects—such as those of fright, anxiety, shame or physical pain may operate as a trauma . . . *as in the case of the apparently irreparable loss of a loved person or because social circumstances made a reaction impossible*"—can be the basis of a neurosis.[72] The latter part of Freud's statement is highly germane to Thérèse, for not only did she suffer from an irreparable loss of a loved one, but also the circumstances surrounding her mother's death militated against an adequate emotional reaction to her loss. "I don't recall having cried very much, neither did I speak to anyone about the feelings I experienced. I looked and listened in silence. No one had any time to pay any attention to me" (S 33).

I will apply Freud's paradigm of the etiology and cure of hysteria contained in *Studies in Hysteria* to Thérèse's illness, not because I'm a Freudian, but because I believe it will help us to make sense out of the scanty information that we have about Thérèse's illness. I originally looked at Thérèse's sickness through the lenses of other psychological paradigms that are more palatable to my taste, but I found that I was cutting the pattern to fit the cloth. To force facts to fit one's pet theory is always a temptation for a writer.

Giving the Devil his Due. Before we look at Thérèse's illness from a psychological perspective, we need to deal with her statement: "The sickness which overtook me certainly came from the demon; infuriated by [Pauline's] entrance into Carmel, he wanted to take revenge on me for the wrong our family was to do him in the future" (S 60). We should not summarily dismiss the demonic as a possible cause of Thérèse's illness as something unworthy of serious consideration. For those of you who find this explanation difficult to believe, I invite you to suspend your judgment, for a good case can be made for the demonic origin of Thérèse's illness based upon two factors: first, the event that triggered her illness; and second, what we know about how the devil operates in the soul.

Thérèse tells us that her sickness began when her uncle evoked memories about her mother. "One evening Uncle took me for a walk and spoke about Mama and about past memories with a kindness that touched me profoundly and made me cry" (S 60). We should not automatically assume that Isidore Guérin's words were the *only* agent that triggered these memories. For the devil operates in the soul primarily in the area of memory and imagination; he brings up emotionally laden images that are buried in our preconscious and unconscious mind. How our psyche and the vast spiritual world intersect one another is an unfathomable mystery. How the saints intercede for us, how their consciousness interpenetrates ours, how we share with them the one life of God, and how the powers of evil have access to the realms of memory and imagination—we do not know. These are phenomena that are shrouded in mystery and cannot be answered by empirical investigation. We can neither *prove* that the origin of Thérèse's illness was diabolical in nature nor should we automatically *dismiss* it. Should we not give some credence to Thérèse's words that the "sickness which overtook [her] certainly came from the demon"? On the other hand, the question has frequently been raised regarding the extent to which these words reflect Thérèse's real feelings. Some contend that they reflect the belief of the Martin family that Thérèse later adopted. In the final analysis, we can only speculate on where the truth lies.

Conversely, for those of you who believe that Thérèse's illness *was* due to the devil, I would urge you not to hold on to your belief too tightly. For the Church herself is very cautious about labeling any phenomenon as demonic in origin until every other possibility—be it physical, emotional, or psychological—has been ruled out. And there are several indications that Thérèse's illness was psychogenic in nature.

Thérèse's Original Intuition. Thérèse's first intuition about the origin of her illness was as follows: "For a long time after my cure . . . I believed I had become ill on purpose" (S 62). Thérèse believed this for years. It was only after she entered Carmel that she received any relief from this thought. Father Almire Pichon, S.J. told her "it was not possible to pretend illness to the extent that [you] have been ill" (S 62). Pichon was right; we cannot *pretend* to be that sick, but we can *make* ourselves that sick if our psyche *chooses* to do so. This is a common phenomenon that I can attest to by personal experience.

A Way Out. There have been times in my life when I was confronted with situations that so filled me with anxiety and dread that all I wanted to do was run away and hide. But I couldn't, for to do so was to become a coward in my own eyes and in the eyes of others. So, how did I solve my dilemma? I became sick. I can recall several times in my life when I made myself sick in order to escape from a situation with which I could not cope. The fear of feeling guilty or ashamed of myself prevented me from making a *conscious* choice, so my *unconscious* made the choice for me. The choice *had* to be made outside of conscious awareness. For even if I possessed the power to snap my fingers and make myself sick, I would have felt guilty because I *knew* what I was doing. But there are no soundproof rooms in our psyche. When we make a choice outside of conscious awareness, the choice *registers* on some level of consciousness, to use Karen Horney's phrase. The registered choice is experienced as a deeply felt intuition, suspicion, hunch, or belief. Such might have been the case with Thérèse. "For a long time after my cure . . . I believed I had become ill on purpose" (S 62).

On Purpose. St. Thomas Aquinas believed that whenever we make a choice, we choose that which we *perceive* to be for our own good. With this as our starting point, what good was Thérèse seeking by choosing (unconsciously) to become sick? Within the context of her life at the time of her illness, the answer to this question is two-fold. She needed to get out of the boarding school, and she wanted Pauline's attention. She could not verbalize her needs, so her sickness spoke for her.

Paradoxically, Thérèse's choice to become sick was a healthy one, for it prevented her from having a mental breakdown. It not only relieved her of the severe mental stress caused by attending boarding school but also provided her with the emotional support that she needed from her family. For example, Céline "would close herself in for hours to be with [me]" (S 64), and "Marie was always by my bedside, taking care of me and consoling me with a mother's tenderness" (S 63). In addition, Thérèse began to receive more consoling letters from Pauline. "My greatest consolation when I was sick was to receive a letter from *Pauline*. I read and reread it until I knew it by heart" (S 64). The letters were medicinal. As Guy Gaucher comments, "The only moments of remission [from her illness] were when Thérèse received a letter from Pauline."[73]

In psychological language, Thérèse's illness fulfilled two types of needs: *primary* gains and *secondary* gains. The primary gain of an illness is what Freud called a *"convenient solution"* to a dilemma; it relieves a person from stress or anxiety without her becoming overwhelmed by guilt. This need was fulfilled by Thérèse's illness because it removed her from the boarding school, and she didn't have to feel guilty because the sickness served as a *legitimate* reason for doing so. Secondary gains provide emotional support from others in the form of sympathy and attention, which Thérèse received from her family. Even though these gains can become addictive, "they sometimes protect a person from disabling neurotic or psychotic development."[74] Such was the case with Thérèse. Her sickness was a *respite,* not an *escape* from the battle of life.

Hysteria. Freud believed that the root cause of hysteria was a *trauma* (which is the Greek word for wound). But why, asked Freud, is an event traumatic for one person and not for another? For example, why was Thérèse traumatized by Zélie's death and Céline was not? It was Freud's belief that it all depends upon "the susceptibility of the person affected."[75] Thérèse was susceptible because of separation experiences from mother figures *prior* to Zélie's death. We now have to ask the question: why is a traumatic event that happened *in the past* the seed for hysteria that will emerge later in life?

Freud's answer to this question may be summed up in T. S. Eliot's words, "Human kind cannot bear very much reality."[76] When a traumatic event is overwhelming, the psyche protects us by creating a distance between ourselves and our feelings by means of what are commonly called *defense mechanisms.* These "inner guardians," as I will call them, function as a protective mother, who shields her child from harm. They shield us from too much reality.

Because of her tender age and previous separations from mother figures, Thérèse needed an inner guardian to protect her from the shock of Zélie's death, a shock that she did not have the capacity to absorb. I believe that the inner guardian that protected Thérèse (one that is commonly employed by scrupulous people like Thérèse) was *isolation,* which "protects the psyche from being overwhelmed by emotions," by barring them from consciousness.⁷⁷ A person who is protected by isolation can often remember *what* has happened without experiencing the attending affect. It is as if one can *see* the video portion of a movie but cannot *hear* the emotionally laden soundtrack. Such seems to have been the case with Thérèse.

In her account of her mother's sickness and death, Thérèse writes: "All the details of my mother's illness are still present to me and I recall especially the last weeks she spent on earth. . . . [but] I don't recall having cried very much, neither did I speak to anyone about the feelings I experienced. I looked and listened in silence" (S 33). Why wouldn't Thérèse cry on the saddest day of her life? Perhaps because she was *incapable* of doing so! Her loss was so great that her tears became frozen in a grief that was too heavy to bear. The inability to cry is often a sign of the deepest state of clinical depression.⁷⁸ As Wordsworth put it, there are "thoughts that do often lie too deep for tears."⁷⁹

The sadness that lies too deep for tears does not dissipate over time. It continues to exist in the unconscious with "freshness and affective strength."⁸⁰ It was these memories "with the whole of their affective coloring . . . [and] the undiminished vividness of a recent event" that began to arise in Thérèse when Uncle Isidore spoke to her about her mother.⁸¹ It was the *emotional intensity* of these memories that overwhelmed Thérèse and precipitated her illness. Or as Freud put it, "Hysterics suffer mainly from reminiscences."⁸²

The night that Thérèse's illness began, she was "seized with a strange trembling" (S 60). This is a manifestation of what Freud called *signal anxiety,* which is the psyche's warning that repressed memories are beginning to break through to consciousness.⁸³ An indication that Thérèse was resisting this process is that she became "fatigued" (S 60), a common symptom of trying to keep the unconscious at bay.

Thérèse's resistance was not only an instinctive reaction but it may also have been an expression of the psyche's innate wisdom in the face of the overwhelming. For when there is a return of repressed content from the unconscious, the personality is threatened by disintegration. At such times, it is wise not to engage the repressed content immediately, but to retreat until one has the strength to encounter it in such a way that it can be integrated into one's personality. As Henry V said when his tired, hungry, ill, and depleted troops were up against an army five times its size, "We would not seek a battle as we are, nor, as we are, we say we shall not shun it" (Henry V. III, vii, 167–68).

This was Thérèse's situation at the time that her repressed memories began to breach her conscious mind. She was depressed and emotionally exhausted from attending boarding school and full of separation anxiety and confusion as the result of Pauline's departure. She was in no position to fight another battle, but neither was she shunning what she eventually had to face. Her sickness was a necessary respite where she could recuperate and gather strength for the battle that lay ahead.

What lay ahead of Thérèse was coming to grips with the death of her mother. The reason why repressed memories come to consciousness with an "undiminished vividness of a *recent* event," is because it is the psyche's "attempt not merely to *relive* an earlier experience, but to *live* it for the *first* time—to live it, that is, with full emotional participation."[84] Thérèse never *fully mourned* her mother's death because she never *fully experienced* it. Psychologically, Zélie's death could not be *past tense* because it was never *present tense*.

But how does one "Pluck from the memory a rooted sorrow; Raze out the written troubles of the brain . . . which weighs upon the heart" (Macbeth V. iii. 51)? Freud's answer to this question was that the rooted sorrow must be given a voice "by allowing the strangulated affect to find a way out through speech."[85] On April 6, 1883, Pauline received the habit. It was this event that brought Thérèse's illness to a crisis and the catalyst that provided her strangulated feelings with a voice.

The Crisis. On the morning of April 6, Thérèse was more ill than usual; yet, shortly before the ceremony she made what seemed like a miraculous recovery. The change was so striking that Thérèse insisted that she "was perfectly cured" (S 62). The extremes of illness and "health" that Thérèse experienced in such a short period of time can be viewed as symptomatic of Thérèse's ambivalence regarding attending the ceremony. Thérèse **desperately wanted to go to the cere**mony not only because she would *see* Pauline but also because she would be able to *touch* her. This is because the ceremony would take place in the chapel outside the cloister. Pauline would come to the chapel dressed as a bride. "I was, then, able to kiss my dear mother, *to sit on her knees* and **give her many** caresses. I was able to contemplate her who was so beautiful under the white adornment of a Bride" (S 61–62). Thérèse was elated because she was able to connect with Pauline, but she knew that what she dreaded the most would soon follow.

Pauline left Thérèse again, but this time *for good*; she returned to the cloister to receive the habit, *never* to return. The grille now became a wall of permanent separation between Thérèse and Pauline. The ceremony that Thérèse so desperately wanted to attend became a source of despair, for it extinguished every vestige of hope that Pauline would ever come home again. "Alas! my trial was only commencing! The next day [after the ceremony] I had another attack similar to the first, and the sickness became so grave that, according to human calculations, I wasn't to recover from it" (S 62).

The Cure. The trial that was commencing for Thérèse involved much more than letting go of her hope that her *second mother* would ever come home; it involved Thérèse's acceptance that her *real mother* was dead. For a month after Pauline's reception of the habit, Thérèse struggled to accept the bitter fact that Zélie was dead. On Pentecost Sunday, on the birthday of the Church, when the Spirit was manifested in tongues of fire, Thérèse's tongue was loosed, her sorrow found its voice, and she was reborn. Here is how Thérèse describes her rebirth:

> One Sunday during the Novena of Masses, Marie went into the garden, leaving me with Léonie who was reading near the window. After a few moments I began calling in a low tone: "Mama, Mama." Léonie, accustomed to hearing me always calling out like this, didn't pay any attention. This lasted a long time, and then I called her much louder. Marie finally returned. I saw her enter, but I cannot say I recognized her and continued to call her in a louder tone: "Mama." I *was suffering very much* from this forced and inexplicable struggle and Marie was suffering perhaps even more than I. After some futile attempts to show me she was by my side, Marie knelt down near my bed with Léonie and Céline. Turning to the Blessed Virgin and praying with the fervor of a mother begging for the life of her child, *Marie* obtained what she wanted.
>
> Finding no help on earth, poor little Thérèse had also turned toward the mother of heaven, and prayed with all her heart that she take pity on her. All of a sudden the Blessed Virgin appeared *beautiful* to me, so *beautiful* that never had I seen anything so attractive; her face was suffused with an ineffable benevolence and tenderness, but what penetrated to the very depths of my soul was the *"ravishing smile of the Blessed Virgin."* At that instant, all my pain disappeared, and

two large tears glistened on my eyelashes, and flowed down my cheeks silently. (S 65–66)

This passage raises many questions. *Who* was Thérèse calling for when she cried "Mama, Mama?" If it was for Marie, then why didn't Thérèse *recognize* her when she came into the room? *Where* was Thérèse? Was she in her bed at Les Buissonnets or was she at her mother's bedside when Zélie was dying? *What* was this *inexplicable struggle?* Was it perhaps Thérèse's strangulated affect that was finally breaking through to consciousness?

So, how are we to interpret Thérèse's cure? Should we look at it as a purely psychological phenomenon devoid of any divine intervention? Our brother Sigmund Freud would say yes. He would argue that the cure was due the psyche's innate drive to make what is unconscious conscious. While I agree with Freud that the psyche, like the body, has an innate tendency to heal itself, this fact alone does not explain *what* was actually taking place in the depths of Thérèse's soul as she was being cured. Was the cure *nothing but* the result of a psychological process? Or was the psyche rather the instrument through which God operated? Were the memories that were triggered in Thérèse's mind nothing but an instance of "free association"? Or was there a Presence that was guiding the process? St. Augustine, in pondering the mysterious regions of the mind where God's providence operates, writes, "God acts upon us . . . where no man has in his own control what shall enter into his thoughts."[86] Not a bad description of free association! Also, is it only by accident that the instrument of Thérèse's cure was the smile of a *mother*?

A Gradual Awakening

THÉRÈSE'S CURE WAS *instantaneous*, but her recovery was *gradual*. Immediately after her cure Thérèse was still highly vulnerable to any form of emotional stress. She suffered some minor relapses. "I upset her twice," said Léonie, "in the months immediately following her cure. She fell down and remained stretched out for several minutes each time; she went completely stiff all over, but this passed of its own accord. On these occasions, however, she did not become delirious or convulsive as she did during her illness."[87]

To aid her convalescence, Louis took Thérèse to Alençon; this was the first time that she had returned to her hometown since Zélie's death. There she revisited the haunts of her childhood, prayed at her mother's grave, and "was entertained, coddled, and admired" (S 73) at the chateaus of her father's upper-middle-class friends. Thérèse found their lifestyle very alluring. "I must admit this type of life had its charms for me. Wisdom is right in saying: '*The bewitching of vanity overturns the innocent mind!*'" (S 73). The lifestyle of her father's friends was bewitching because it was able "to ally the joys of this earth to the service of God" (S 73). Its aesthetically pleasing chateau existence draped over with pious religiosity easily counterfeited the peace of God. It was a worldly spirituality "where leveled lawns and gravelled ways / Where slippered Contemplation finds his ease / And Childhood a delight for every sense, / But takes our greatness with our violence."[88]

This bourgeois life of slippered contemplation was tempting for Thérèse. It not only held charms for her but offered protection from her fears. How easy it would have been for Thérèse to stay within the protective walls of the family circle. Thérèse could have remained daddy's little girl all of her life, staying at Les Buissonnets, living a quiet, pious life, and accompanying her father, arm in arm, on various pilgrimages across Europe.

The grace that Thérèse received during her weeks in Alençon was the beginning of a sobering realization that would come to fruition three years later at her "Christmas conversion." At Alençon, Thérèse began to see what she *might have become* if she had never grown up—an adult who remained a child. When Thérèse returned to Lisieux, two events occurred that deepened this realization.

The first event happened during the three days she lived at the boarding school in preparation for her First Communion.

> In the morning, I found it very nice to see all the students getting up so early and doing the same as they; but I was not yet accustomed to taking care of myself. *Marie* was not there to comb and *curl* my hair, and so I was obliged to go and timidly offer my comb to the mistress in charge of the dressing rooms. She laughed at seeing a big girl of eleven not knowing how to take care of herself. . . . During my retreat I became aware that I was really a child who was fondled and cared for like few other children on earth, especially among those deprived of their mothers. (S 75)

The solicitous love that Thérèse's family lavished upon her was *necessary* because of her emotional fragileness; nevertheless, it was *overprotective*. Thérèse may have needed to bury "her fragile roots in *a chosen soil*" (S 53) in order to survive, but it also kept her a child. At the boarding school, Thérèse came to this realization. Yes, she had lost her mother, but so had many of her peers. Yet she was different from them, for she was "fondled and cared for like few other children on earth, especially among those deprived of their mothers." Thérèse was beginning the most difficult battle that she would ever have to fight—leaving the security of the family nest—in short, growing up! The consequences of not growing up came home to Thérèse in 1886 when she began to be tutored by Madame Papinau.[89] Several times a week, Thérèse went to Madame Papinau's home for instruction. Madame Papinau, who was "a little old-maidish in her ways" (S 85), lived with her mother. "When I arrived, I usually found only old lady Cochain [the mother] who looked at me '*with her big clear eyes*' and then called out in a calm, sententious voice: '*Mme. Pâpineau . . . Ma . . . d'môizelle Thêrèse est là! . . .*' Her daughter answered promptly in an *infantile* voice: 'Here I am, *Mama*'" (S 85). The two words that Thérèse emphasized in Madame Papinau's response are *infantile* and *Mama*. Thérèse is viewing the type of person she might have become if she had not chosen to leave home—an adult woman who had remained a little girl. Also, while Thérèse was receiving her lessons in Madame Papinau's "antiquely furnished room," old lady Cochain was engaged in chitchat with "all types of persons: priests, ladies, young girls, etc." (S 85).

These details that Thérèse records, the interchange between Madame Papinau and her mother, the antiquely furnished room, and the incessant front parlor chatter of old lady Cochain are not inconsequential. Together, they painted a frightening self-portrait for Thérèse of what she could have become, for her lifestyle was tending in that direction.

While Thérèse was taking lessons from Madame Papinau, she had set herself up in Pauline's old attic studio. "Since my leaving the boarding school, I set myself up in *Pauline's* old painting room and arranged it to suit my taste. It was a real bazaar, an assemblage of pious objects and curiosities, a garden, and an aviary, . . . [and] enthroned all by itself the portrait of *Pauline* at the age of ten. . . . [This was] 'my museum'" (S 90). It is hard to imagine that a precociously intelligent child like Thérèse did not see, reflected in her "museum" of knickknacks in which a portrait of her "second mother" was *enthroned*, an image of Madame Papinau's relationship to her mother in her "antiquely furnished room" with its suffocating palaver.

Madame Papinau was a foreboding omen for Thérèse, a prophetic warning of the type of woman she might become if she did not begin to grow up. Thérèse took this warning to heart. She began to change her behavior. "I wasn't accustomed to doing things for myself. Céline tidied up the room in which we slept, and I myself didn't do any housework whatsoever. After Marie's entrance into Carmel, it sometimes happened that I tried to make up the bed to please God, or else in the evening, when Céline was away, I'd bring in her plants" (S 97). Even though these were baby steps, they should not be despised as insignificant, for any change in the right direction is important. Nevertheless, the greatest catalyst for change was her insight into her *emotional overreaction* when her efforts were not recognized by Céline. "If Céline was unfortunate enough not to seem happy or surprised because of these little services, I became unhappy and proved it by my tears. I really was unbearable because of my extreme touchiness. . . . I really don't know how I could entertain the thought of entering Carmel when I was still in the *swaddling clothes of a child!*" (S 97).

Reality was beginning to sink in for Thérèse. We can almost hear her thinking: "My family has been very tolerant of my overreactions to little things; God bless them for their patience. But here I am, going on fourteen, thinking of entering a community of adult women who are not going to wipe my nose or change my diapers but will expect me to act like an adult. I need to gain control of my emotions. After being pampered by my family and being Papa's 'little queen' all of my life, it will be very difficult for me not to make my feelings the center of the universe. If there is anything in my life that I need, it is for God to restore the strength of soul that I lost when my mother died." Thérèse received this grace at her "Christmas conversion," which we will explore in the next chapter. For now, let us focus on what we can learn from Thérèse's overreaction.

Why was Thérèse hurt when Céline was neither surprised nor overjoyed on seeing the "little services" that she had performed? Was it not because Thérèse was *expecting* to be praised? Was it not because she *expected* Céline to make a "big deal" out of her little services? Isn't this true for all of us? Namely, when people's reactions do not measure up to what we *expect* them to be, or what we *want* them to be, or even what we *need* them to be, we can become either crestfallen or angry at their "insensitivity." In this regard, Charles Dickens gives us an example from his own life.

Shortly before writing *Great Expectations*, Dickens visited his hometown of Chatham and walked about town visiting the haunts of his boyhood. One day, as he meandered about, he spied the greengrocer whom he had known as a child. Excited, Dickens introduced himself and shared the fond memories that he held of playing in front of the grocery store when he was a child. But Dickens was taken aback when the grocer did not respond as he had expected:

> He was not in the least excited or gratified or in any way roused, by the accuracy of my recollection. . . . Nettled by this phlegmatic conduct, I informed him that I had left the town when I was a child. He slowly returned, quite unsoftened, and not without a sarcastic kind of complacency, "*Had*

I? Ah! And did I find it had got on tolerably well without me?" Such is the difference, I thought, when I had left him a few hundred yards behind, and was by so much in a better temper, between going away from a place and remaining in it. I had no right, I reflected, to be angry with the greengrocer for his want of interest, I was nothing to him: whereas he was the town, the cathedral, the bridge, the river, my childhood, and a large slice of my life, to me.[90]

This incident in Dickens' life is often reenacted in our own. How often do we feel put down by or even take offense at someone who does not mirror back to us our joy or enthusiasm about some pet project or success that we have had? When I was in the process of writing my first book, I shared this new venture with a friend. Her response was, "What's the subject matter?" I was deflated. I expected her to say something like, "A book, you're writing a book! Wow, that's fantastic!" And like Dickens, I had no reason to be hurt, but I was. Yet the only reason I felt *deflated* was because my ego was *inflated*.

Now that I am at a distance from that conversation, I can see that my friend took a genuine interest in my work. She did not change the subject matter as often happens in the course of conversation. Rather, she took time to ask me many questions about my writing. For example, how was I going to approach my subject matter? What slant was I going to take? Her response was not perfunctory, but I perceived it to be so because I *expected* her to respond with the same degree of emotion as *I* felt about my work. I could not perceive her interest, for I was too absorbed in my hurt feelings, too preoccupied in licking my wounded ego.

Just as the pain of my bruised ego labeled my friend's response as a sign of her indifference, so too does any type of pain have the tendency to misinterpret and distort the actions and motives of those around us. For our emotions shape and color the lenses through which we see life. This is most true when we are experiencing an insufferable loss.

Think of a time when you have lost a loved one through death, be it your best friend, your spouse, a sibling or, God forbid, your child. You are beside yourself with grief. Your friends come to the wake to offer their condolences. And one of them, after sitting with you for a while, says, "I wish I could stay longer but I need to go." You say, "Of course, I understand." But you don't. How can *anything* be more important than being with you at this time? It is emotionally unimaginable that your friend hasn't put his or her life on hold because of your loss. When our life has been shattered, it is hard to even imagine how the world can continue to go about on its merry way.

The reality that life goes on around us in the midst of our personal tragedies is portrayed in Bruegel's painting *Landscape with the Fall of Icarus*. It depicts a serene pastoral scene on a beautiful spring day. In the foreground is a farmer absorbed in plowing a field on a hillside and a shepherd contemplating the unfolding green of the season, while down below a ship in full sail calmly glides upon a sparkling sea. But in the midst of this idyllic scene is a small detail that the viewer may easily overlook—two small white legs disappearing into the sea. The legs are those of Icarus, the youth who flew too high and plunged to his death in the sea when the heat of the sun melted the wax that held fast the feathers of his wings.[91]

Bruegel's juxtaposition of people going about their daily tasks as human tragedy unfolds nearby has given rise to much reflection. In 1938, after seeing Bruegel's painting, W. H. Auden wrote *Musée des Beaux Arts*.

About human suffering they were never wrong,
The Old Masters: how well they understood
Its human position; how it takes place
While someone else is eating or opening a window or just
    walking dully along . . .
In Breughel's *Icarus,* for instance; how everything turns away
Quite leisurely from the disaster; the ploughman may
Have heard the splash, the forsaken cry,
But for him it was not an important failure; the sun shone
As it had to on the white legs disappearing into the green
Water, and the expensive delicate ship must have seen
Something amazing, a boy fall out of the sky, but
Had somewhere to get to and sailed calmly on.[92]

"In three words I can sum up everything I've ever learned," said Robert Frost. "Life goes on." We all know that this is true, but it is a difficult truth to bear when *we* are the Icarus in life's drama, and people have "somewhere to get to." Or even worse, when our personal tragedies are not even noticed. As William Carlos Williams put it in his poem *Landscape with the Fall of Icarus,* our rack and ruin, our personal tragedy or undoing, is but "a splash quite unnoticed."[93] It is a fact. The world turns away from our anguish, has somewhere to get to when we are sitting in our pain. It doesn't enthusiastically applaud our successes, but simply says "that's nice," and rarely gives recognition to our best efforts to be good.

These facts of life can make us cynical. Or they can be invitations to a stance of "humbling indifference," as psychologist James Hillman wrote, commenting upon Auden's poem.[94] It is a very deflating but redemptive experience to realize that one is not the center of the universe. Thérèse's hypersensitivity, coupled with her years of being treated with kid gloves by her family, made it very difficult for her to accept that the world did not revolve around her feelings.

The gradual awakening that life goes on was a great grace for Thérèse. It was the requisite grace of her "Christmas conversion," when she was given the strength to get on with her life.

The Battle of Bearing Her Emotions

THE "THIRD PERIOD" of Thérèse's life dawned on December 25, 1886, when God gave her the grace to control her "extreme touchiness" (S 97). Thérèse said it was the greatest grace that she had ever received. It restored the strength of soul that she had lost when her mother died. The centrality of Thérèse's Christmas conversion cannot be overemphasized. It was *the* event that changed the entire course of her life. It was the moment when she "received the grace of leaving . . . childhood" (S 98).

The Event. On Christmas day, it was a French tradition to fill the shoes of the baby of the family with little gifts. This custom continued in the Martin household until Thérèse was fourteen. When the Martin family returned home after attending midnight Mass in 1886, Louis noticed Thérèse's shoes in front of the fireplace and sighed to Céline, "Thérèse ought to have outgrown all this sort of thing, and I hope this will be the last time."[95]

Céline caught Thérèse's eye and realized that she had overheard her father's remark. Aware of Thérèse's hypersensitivity, Céline followed her upstairs and found Thérèse sitting on her bed, her eyes filled with tears. Céline told her not to go downstairs in this state. Thérèse recounts:

> I was no longer the same; Jesus had changed [my] heart! Forcing back my tears, I descended the stairs rapidly;

controlling the poundings of my heart, I took my slippers and placed them in front of Papa, and withdrew all the objects joyfully. I had the happy appearance of a queen. Having regained his own cheerfulness, Papa was laughing; Céline believed it was all a *dream*! Fortunately, it was a sweet reality; Thérèse had discovered once again the strength of soul which she had lost at the age of four and a half, and she was to preserve it forever! On that *night of light* began the third period of my life." (S 98)

Here is an account of a teenage girl choosing to control her feelings. A seemingly insignificant event; yet it was the turning point in Thérèse's life. God "made me *strong* and courageous, arming me with His weapons. Since that night I have never been defeated in any combat. . . . The source of my tears was dried up . . . [and I received] the grace of leaving my childhood, in a word, the grace of my complete conversion" (S 97–98).

Leaving Childhood. What does it mean to leave childhood? What does it mean to become an adult? It means having the strength not to be ruled by one's emotions or allowing one's feelings to dictate one's choices and possessing the determination to stand upright in the face of an emotional storm. This was the grace given to Thérèse.

Thérèse was *not* healed of her hypersensitivity. Rather, she was given the *strength* to deal with it. Her father's remark deeply hurt Thérèse, but she received the strength not to give in to her tears. Her *feelings* were not *changed*; rather, she was given the *strength* to *control* them: "*Forcing back* my tears . . . [and] *controlling* the poundings of my heart" (S 98, emphases added).

The grace that Thérèse received from "the *strong* and *powerful God*" was "the *strength* of soul which she had lost" (S 98, emphases modified). God did not *remove* Thérèse from the battle of her emotions but gave her the fortitude to remain *in* the battle. "It is God's will that I fight right up until death" (LC 38). Pauline testified that "In Carmel [Thérèse] was just as sensitive as others . . . and found people just as annoying."[96] When Thérèse was sitting on her bed, her eyes filled with tears, she knew that God had "armed" her to do combat. And when she *chose* to enter the battle, "the third period" of her life began. "Since that night I have never been defeated in any combat" (S 97).

The Combat. The battle that Thérèse engaged in on December 25, 1886, was the form of *all* the battles that she would fight. Whether it was the battle to endure her "natural antipathy" toward Sister Teresa of St. Augustine (S 222), the courage to face her fears when she was appointed novice mistress, the patience to suffer boredom while listening to Sister St. Raphael drone on and on delivering spiritual nosegays, the fortitude to work with Sister Marie of St. Joseph in the linen closet, the capacity to bear up under her father's mental illness, the grace to deal with her scrupulosity, or the strength to resist being mothered by Pauline and other mother figures in Carmel, the battle was the same. It was the battle of bearing her emotions.

Reflect upon your own life, my dear readers. What do we suffer in doing God's will? Is it not some painful emotion that accompanies our choices? Is it not fear that makes an act of faith harrowing? Is it not the sadness of mourning that makes "letting go" difficult? Is not loneliness or emptiness the price of remaining faithful to one's vows? Is not tediousness and boredom the burden of being dutiful to the daily round?

Love and suffering are inseparable. If we are unwilling to suffer, then we cannot love. The grace of her Christmas conversion gave Thérèse the strength to embrace this truth. And it revealed to her that true happiness lies in love. "I felt *charity* enter into my soul, and the need to forget myself and to please others; since then I've been happy" (S 99). If we do not understand this truth, then we cannot understand what Thérèse meant when she said that she *loved suffering*. Thérèse was not in love with pain; she was in love with God. Her love for God expressed itself in her choices to love her neighbor. This demanded that she bear the pain that love entails. By embracing suffering, she experienced the embrace of God. If God is love, then we cannot know God by any other means than love. There is no truth in those who claim that they *know* God without *loving* their neighbor (1 Jn 2:4).

The Nature of Healing. Freud once said that therapy ends when we are dealing with our problems and they are no longer dealing with us. Thirty-five years ago, when I was a gung-ho undergraduate psychology major, Freud's viewpoint sounded pessimistic and depressing. Now, as a man in his sixties who is still struggling with the same fears and neurotic tendencies that I wrestled with in my youth, I see Freud's perspective as being realistic. For are not our deeply rooted, deeply embedded, and deeply entrenched personality traits chronic, obdurate, and unyielding by definition?

Even though I believe that by the grace of God I am not the man I was thirty-five years ago, for I can honestly say that much emotional healing has taken place in my heart. Nevertheless, during times of stress when my old fears and neurotic compulsions well up within me in all their savage intensity, I feel that nothing has changed. I say to myself, "When will I ever be rid of this fear?"

Once I could accept the answer "*Never*" I felt a great weight taken off my shoulders. For I was released from the impossible goal of trying to become someone other than myself. "Working on yourself" can be an insidious mask of self-hate, for it makes you feel that there is something wrong with you until you are "healed."

I have often told people who come to me for spiritual direction to never make it a goal to conquer their faults. Simply ask for the grace to resist the temptation of the moment. Take it for granted that you will always have tendencies toward certain sins and self-destructive behaviors, which will always be opportunities to grow in virtue and rely upon the grace of God.

"I had no need to grow up" (S 208). Thérèse did not make it a goal to get *beyond* the effects of her childhood but to do the will of God *in the midst* of them. Thérèse understood that the emotional wounds of her childhood were not obstacles to spiritual growth but the *context* of growing in holiness.

Thérèse can help us to refocus our goal in life. She tells us to keep our minds on *doing* the will of God. If our emotions are transformed in the process, all well and good. Praise God! But if they are not changed, they are the context in which we will grow in God's love.

The Martyrdom of Scruples

In Hans Christian Andersen's story *The Princess and the Pea*, a young damsel who professes to be a real princess arrives at the entrance of a castle one stormy night seeking shelter. The prince of the castle is overjoyed because he has been searching for a true princess to be his wife. But the queen is skeptical of the damsel's claim. So, in order to ascertain the validity of her pronouncement, the queen hurries to the guest room, strips the bed of its bedclothes and places a small pea on the bed board and covers it with twenty mattresses and twenty eiderdown quilts. "In the morning, when someone asked the princess how she had slept, she responded, 'Oh, just wretchedly! I didn't close my eyes once, the whole night. . . . God knows what was in that bed; it was something hard.' . . . Now they knew that she was a real princess. . . . For only a real princess could be so sensitive!"[97]

Andersen's story can serve as a metaphor for a *sensitive conscience* or a highly developed spiritual consciousness that is so delicate, sensitive, and finely attuned to the presence of God that it instinctively knows when something is *not* of God. As Andersen's story symbolizes, a sensitive conscience is a heightened state of consciousness—a manifestation of the soul's true nobility.

Carl Jung held that the soul is *aristocratic* by nature, that is, it instinctively strives to be ruled by the best within itself (from the Latin *aristocratia*, which means: government by the best).[98] Saints are ruled by the best that they find within themselves. Seeing their face reflected in the unclouded mirror of

God's countenance, they are highly sensitive to their imperfections. "O noble conscience, clear and undefaced," cries Dante, "How keen thy self-reproach for one small slip!"[99] Thérèse had a sensitive conscience that pricked her when she felt herself veering from the will of God. She "[felt] that [God was] within [her], at each moment; guiding and inspiring [her] with what to say and do" (S 179). But Thérèse's sensitive conscience was infected by scruples.

Scrupulosity is an extremely painful anxiety disorder. It consists of a gnawing fear that one has offended God or could offend God at any moment and that God will cast her into hell. To protect herself from eternal damnation, the scrupulous person dissects every thought, motive, and action in order to ascertain if she has sinned. And since she is deathly afraid that she *might* have sinned, the scrupulous person seeks *absolute certitude* that she hasn't sinned in order to assuage her fears.

Ironically, the certitude that the scrupulous person seeks *sustains* the fears she hopes to *assuage*. This is because the quest for absolute certitude engenders obsessive doubting. Just when the scrupulous person feels that she has obtained absolute certitude that she has not sinned, a nagging voice whispers, "But are you sure?" This doubt revives her fears and the dissecting of thoughts and motives commences a never-ending cycle.[100]

In obsessive-compulsive disorders (of which scrupulosity is a species), an *obsession* is an intrusive, unremitting thought, impulse, or idea that causes anxiety; a *compulsion* is an action that alleviates the anxiety. For example, a man leaves his home in the morning and as he is driving to work the thought arises, "Did I unplug the coffee pot?" To relieve his anxiety, the man returns home. When he finds that the coffee pot is unplugged, his anxiety is relieved. He gets back into his car and continues to drive to work. But then the thought arises, "But are you *sure* that you unplugged the coffee pot?" This renewed anxiety compels him to go home again. Again, he is relieved when he finds that the coffee pot is unplugged. And on and on and on. Obsessive checking becomes addictive because it temporarily relieves anxiety. As a result, the obsessive-compulsive becomes trapped in an *anxiety-relief* cycle.

When Thérèse was twelve and a half years old, she was caught in an *anxiety-relief* cycle for eighteen months when she became infected by scruples. Every time Thérèse believed that any of her thoughts or actions were slightly sinful, she would run to Marie to get certitude that she had not sinned. When Marie assured Thérèse that she had not sinned, Thérèse's anxiety was allayed, but only until the doubt "But are you sure?" flashed through her mind. "As soon as I laid down my burden [by telling Marie of my fears], I experienced peace for an instant; but this peace passed away like a lightning flash, and soon my martyrdom began over again. What patience my dear Marie needed to listen to me without showing any annoyance" (S 84–85). Let us now explore the causes of Thérèse's scrupulosity and how scrupulosity impacted the rest of her life.

Jansenism, the Remote Cause of Thérèse's Scrupulosity. There lurks in the mind of a scrupulous person the specter of a wrathful God. Such a God, in the guise of Jansenism, haunted nineteenth-century France. Jansenism was a heresy that emphasized the depravity of human nature and its inclination toward sin. It preached a divine justice that was so stern and exacting that only a few people were saved. It taught that sacramental absolution did not forgive sins but only declared them forgiven to the person who already possessed the perfect love of God. Likewise, Jansenism held that it was only the unsullied soul, free of all taint of sin, that could approach the Communion rail without the fear of committing a sacrilege. Jansenistic piety was excessively rigid, moralistic, and rooted in an image of God as a harsh judge of unyielding justice. Jansenism held that the possibility of committing a mortal sin was an ever-present and constant danger. These beliefs gave rise to the excessive introspection that was the seedbed and breeding ground of scrupulosity. Jansenism tainted the pulpit and Catholic pedagogy, which in turn infected the faithful.

Thérèse's family was not immune to this infection. We see it manifested in Zélie's excessive fear of sin and hell. For example, Zélie was terrified that her five-year-old daughter Hélene was in purgatory, or perhaps even in hell, because she once told a lie. As extreme and irrational as Zélie's fear may seem to us, it is understandable in the light of her Jansenistic upbringing. In the *Summarium* for Zélie's beatification, we read that the Guérin home was dominated by "a certain atmosphere of austerity, constraint and scrupulosity."[101] "[Zélie's mother] who taught her daughters an excessive fear of offending God, used to harp on the phrase 'that's a sin' to curb the least imperfections."[102] Zélie's sister Marie-Louise "had feared to commit the grave sin of finding herself near a little boy. She would slip away trembling, as skillfully as possible, sometimes bringing malicious teasing upon herself because of what others interpreted as her wild temperament."[103]

Similarly, Madame Guérin, was "too austere" with Zélie and treated her "so harshly" that Zélie's childhood was "as sad as a winding sheet [a shroud]."[104] In addition to the Jansenistic atmosphere of the Guérin household, the lack of parental bonding between Zélie and her mother may have been one of the chief causes of Zélie's depressive personality which contributed to her scrupulosity. Depression both triggers and aggravates obsessional thinking, a chief characteristic of scrupulosity.[105]

But whatever the case may have been, Zélie exhibited symptoms of scrupulosity similar to those of her sister Marie-Louise. For example, Zélie trembled with fear on her wedding night when she discovered what conjugal relations involved. To us who live in a different world than the one that Zélie was raised in, Zélie's ignorance of the facts of life and the emotional trauma that she experienced on her wedding night may strike us as incredible, but her ignorance is completely understandable when we realize that in her world sex was shrouded in an awful silence. And her terror of conjugal relations was *proportionate* to the fear of damnation that was connected with anything having to do with sex.[106] We will never know what transpired in the hearts of Zélie and Louis or of the exchange that took place between them on their marriage night, except that they agreed to live as brother and sister (a "Josephite marriage"). Céline writes, "In her letters, mother has stated that before marriage she was ignorant of the mysteries of life, and that when she learned them she was troubled, even to tears. Father profited by this circumstance to propose to her his own project of their living together as brother and sister. She agreed to this, in spite of her former desire to have children."[107]

How are we to interpret the above passage? Was Louis's proposal a compassionate and sensitive response to his wife's fears, or was he taking advantage of the situation in order to live out what he held to be an ideal? Biographers have come down on both sides of this question. Also, was Zélie *relieved* by Louis's proposal because it allayed her fears of having sex, or was she *resentful* because he put her in a position where she was forced to choose between calming her anxiety and frustrating her desire to have children? I suspect that *all* of the above are true. Louis and Zélie were not cardboard figures but real, complex human beings. They lived together as brother and sister for ten months, but Zélie's desire to have children was greater than her fear. The rest is history.

Thérèse's Scrupulosity. In what ways and to what degree Thérèse was infected by the Jansenistic atmosphere of her culture and her home life is open to speculation. For example, how would you interpret the following passages? When Thérèse was three and a half, Zélie wrote the following to Pauline regarding Thérèse:

> She becomes emotional very easily. As soon as she does anything wrong, everybody must know about it. Yesterday, not meaning to do so, she tore off a small piece of wallpaper. She wanted to tell her father immediately, and you would have pitied her to see her anxiety. When he returned four hours later and everybody had forgotten about it, she ran at once to Marie, saying: "Marie, hurry and tell Papa I tore the paper." Then she awaited her sentence as if she were a criminal. There is an idea in her little head that if she owns up to something, she will be more readily forgiven. (S 18–19)

A year later Marie wrote to Pauline: "[Thérèse] is very sensitive; when she's said a word too many, or when she's made a mistake, she notices it immediately and, to make up for it, the poor baby has recourse to tears, and she asks for pardons which never end. We tell her she's forgiven but in vain. She goes on crying just the same" (L 114).

Do these passages give evidence that Thérèse possessed a *sensitive* conscience beyond her youthful years? Considering that Thérèse was a precociously intelligent, reflective, and observant child, we may answer in the affirmative. But do these passages not *also* indicate an incipient scrupulosity insofar as they manifest three common characteristics of scrupulous persons? First, Thérèse exhibits an excessive fear of being punished for any transgression. Second, Thérèse labels as sinful actions that are not sinful; she felt extremely guilty over actions that were accidents and mistakes. Third, Thérèse found it difficult to believe that she was forgiven *after* forgiveness had been granted to her.

Do these passages indicate a sensitive or scrupulous conscience? No one knows. But in this author's opinion they suggest both. Thérèse was highly *attuned* to God's presence early in life, but she was also highly *impressionable* to the world around her. And it was the impress of the Jansenistic world upon Thérèse's psyche that made her vulnerable to a major attack of scruples.

An Attack of Scruples. What follows is a description of hell found in a retreat conference in James Joyce's *Portrait of the Artist as a Young Man*:

> Let us try for a moment to realize the abode of the damned which the justice of an offended God has called into existence for the eternal punishment of sinners. Hell is a strait and dark and foul smelling prison, an abode of demons and lost souls, filled with fire and smoke. The straitness of this prison house is expressly designed by God to punish [sinners]. [In hell], by reason of their great number, the prisoners are heaped together in their awful prison, the walls of which are said to be four thousand miles thick: and the damned are so utterly bound and helpless that they are not even able to remove from the eye a worm that gnaws it. The horror of this dark prison is increased by its awful stench. All the filth of the world, all the offal and scrum of the world shall run there as to a vast reeking sewer and the bodies of the damned exhale such a pestilential odour that one of them alone would suffice to infect the whole world. Imagine some foul and putrid corpse that has lain rotting and decomposing in

the grave, a jellylike mass of liquid corruption. Imagine such a corpse a prey of flames, devoured by the fire of burning brimstone and giving off dense choking fumes of nauseous loathsome decomposition. And then imagine this sickening stench, multiplied a millionfold and a millionfold again from the millions upon millions of fetid carcasses massed together in the reeking darkness, a huge and rotting human fungus. Imagine all this and you will have some idea of the horror of the stench of hell. . . .

[Then the devils] mock and jeer at the lost souls. Why did you sin? Why did you not leave that evil companion? Why did you not give up that lewd habit, that impure habit? Yes, a just God who metes out an everlasting and infinite punishment in the fires of hell for a single grievous sin. [But] even a venial sin is of such foul and hideous nature that even if the omnipotent Creator could end all the evil and misery in the world, the wars, the diseases, the robberies, the crimes, the deaths, the murders, on condition that He allowed a single venial sin to pass unpunished, a single venial sin, a lie, be it in thought or deed, is a transgression of His law and God would not be God if He did not punish the transgressor.[108]

This excerpt from James Joyce's novel *A Portrait of the Artist as a Young Man* captures the flavor of what Thérèse must have heard during the retreat that she had made in preparation of her renewal of her First Communion in May 1885 when she was twelve-and-a-half-years old. On the bottom of the souvenir given to each girl who made this retreat was written: "Better to die than to sully one's soul with a mortal sin." The titles of the retreat conferences that Thérèse heard were: Hell, Judgment, Mortal Sin, The Necessity of Making a Good Confession, and Sacrilegious Communion. "What M. l'Abbé [Domin] told us was frightening," wrote Thérèse in her retreat notes. "He spoke about mortal sin, and he described a soul in the state of sin and how much God hated it" (L 226).

Thérèse's fear triggered an agonizing attack of scruples that lasted for the next eighteen months. "One would have to pass through this martyrdom to understand it well, and for me to express what I suffered for a *year and a half* would be impossible. All my most simple thoughts and actions became the cause of trouble for me, and I had relief only when I told them to Marie. This cost me dearly, for I believed I was obliged to tell her the absurd thoughts I had even about her" (S 84). Thérèse's choice of the word *martyrdom* is not an expression of a histrionic schoolgirl but an accurate description of the torment that scrupulosity inflicts upon its victims. A forty-four-year-old married schoolteacher who suffers from scruples says, "Many times my thoughts have no reason. When I have obsessive sexual thoughts, I wonder if this is a sin. I have such a hard time distinguishing between a fantasy and an intention." In the same vein, a twenty-four-year-old computer programmer writes, "What worries me is that at any moment and in only a few seconds I could commit a serious sin. The only remedy is confession. I worry about what I've done until I confess it; then it's all over. The problem is that I fall or worry again and need to go back."[109] These two testimonies may provide us with understanding why Thérèse's "most simple thoughts and actions became the cause of trouble for [her] and [she] had relief only when [she] told them to Marie."

Let us recall that a scrupulous person seeks absolute certitude that she has not sinned. Now, put yourself in the mind of a highly reflective twelve-year-old girl who is deathly afraid that any thought may be a serious sin. How do you, how *can* you distinguish between fantasy and intention? Where is the thin line of demarcation between partial consent and full consent? And how does a person who is terrified that the possibility of eternal damnation is an ever-present danger shut down her harried, worried, careworn mind and find relief? She can't!

The question now arises: did the content of Thérèse's scruples have to do with sex? We don't know. We know by Thérèse's own testimony that she never had any problems in the area of sexual temptation. But this does not mean that her bout with scruples did not revolve around sexuality. For we are not dealing with temptation but *confusion*.

The source of Thérèse's confusion that may have triggered her bout with scruples were all the hormonal, physiological and emotional changes that were transpiring within her as a result of puberty. Thérèse was twelve and a half during her second Communion retreat. It is important to note that Thérèse's First Communion retreat, *which she made a year earlier*, did not trigger a crisis in scruples. And this retreat was also given by Father Domin, who spoke on the same hell and brimstone subjects that he did the following year. One can almost hear Thérèse saying to herself, "Are these strange bodily sensations and feelings that I'm experiencing against the sixth commandment, sins which Father Domin told us God abhors?" And if there is any state of mind that a scrupulous person finds anxiety-ridden, it is ambiguity. For ambiguity deprives the scrupulous person of what he or she so desperately desires—absolute certitude that he or she has not sinned.

Thérèse could not obtain the certitude that she wanted but only obtained temporary relief by having a trusted authority figure tell her that she had not sinned. Marie was this person. "It was especially on the eve of her confessions that they [Thérèse's scruples] recurred. She came to tell me all of her so-called sins. I tried to cure her by telling her that I took her sins upon myself (they were not even imperfections) and by allowing her to confess only two or three of them, which I indicated to her myself."[110] This testimony of Marie is very significant because it gives us a clue regarding the nature of Thérèse's scruples.

A common misconception that can be easily drawn about Thérèse's scrupulosity from reading *Story of a Soul* is that Thérèse had no respite from her scruples during the eighteen-month period that followed the retreat that she had made in May 1885. This is not true. For in July of the same year, Thérèse had a very joyous time with her aunt at Saint-Ouen followed by a two-week holiday at the seashore in Trouville. "Thérèse is delightfully happy," wrote Madame Guérin to her husband. "Mama [Madame Fournet, Céline Guérin's mother] was telling me yesterday that she had never seen Thérèse so gay, with her face so frankly happy. Yesterday, she and Marie came home all decked out in little bouquets. Marie had cornflowers, Thérèse had forget-me-nots. All was perfectly arranged. They were wearing their Breton aprons, with well-made bouquets at each of the corners, on their heads, at the end of their pigtails, and even on their shoes" (L 228–29).

Just as Abbé Domin communicated to Thérèse the stern God of Jansenism, so did nature speak to Thérèse of God's beauty and love. "A feature of [Thérèse's] piety that struck me particularly," testified Thérèse's novice mistress, "because I had never heard it spoken of in Carmel or in the lives of the saints, was the role she attributed to flowers. For her, *every flower spoke a language of its own, in which revealed God's infinite love and perfections to her. She also used them to tell God of her own love and other sentiments.*"[111] Thérèse could have fully resonated with Wordsworth's belief that nature has the power to inform our minds and touch our hearts.

> Knowing that nature never did betray
> The heart that loved her; 'tis her privilege,
> Through all the years of this our life, to lead
> From joy to joy: for she can so inform
> The mind that is within us, so impress
> With quietness and beauty, and so feed
> With lofty thoughts, that neither evil tongues,
> Rash judgments, nor the sneers of selfish men,
> Nor greetings where no kindness is, nor all
> The dreary intercourse of daily life,
> Shall e'er prevail against us, or disturb
> Our cheerful faith that all which we behold
> Is full of blessings.[112]

However, Thérèse's cheerful faith in a loving God who spoke to her through every flower could not completely protect her from the mirthless God of Jansenism. "I remember the joy I had putting on some pretty sky-blue ribbons Aunt had given me for my hair; I also recall having confessed at Trouville even this childish pleasure which seemed to be a sin to me" (S 89). The joy of being in the presence of a loving God, which was periodically overshadowed by the specter of the judgmental God of Jansenism, may serve as a symbol of how Thérèse was affected by scrupulosity all her life. Thérèse *believed* in a merciful God but this does not mean that she always *felt* that God was merciful.

One might think that a monastery would prove to be a safe haven from the God of Jansenism, but this was not the case with Thérèse for the spirituality of Lisieux Carmel had been infected by the heresy of her age. I say infected because the underlying vision of the vocation of a Carmelite nun that was held by Lisieux Carmel was essentially good. It was rooted in the theology of the Mystical Body of Christ, which taught that since we are all connected to one another in Christ, then any sacrifice or act of love done by an individual positively affects all the members of the body. This is the theology that undergirds St. Teresa's teaching that prayer is apostolic by nature. Unfortunately, Jansenism distorted this vision.

> The apostolic doctrine of the French Carmel is contained fully in the notion by which a Carmelite nun is put in the place of a sinner, acting as a substitute. By her very calling, the Carmelite nun is a victim offered to God in order to offset the obstinacy of the sinner . . . to appease the justice of God by willingly accepting the punishments due to sinners. When this plan was taken literally, the fidelity of the nun to her calling was judged according to the intensity of her spiritual and bodily mortifications. This was the ideal in favor at the Carmel of Lisieux under the government of Mère Marie de Gonzague. The cross of iron and the whip of nettles were then held in high honor. It was thought that thus might necessary sacrifices be offered to the justice of God, and merit piled up for those who worked for the upbuilding of his Kingdom.[113]

This was the corporate vision of the group that Thérèse entered at the age of fifteen. They saw themselves as human "lightening rods" that deflected the wrath of God from sinners, the same God that triggered Thérèse's crisis of scruples at the age of twelve. This is an extremely significant fact in our understanding of Thérèse's life in Carmel.

Try to place yourself in Thérèse's position. You're a teenage girl susceptible to self-doubt, who was once so terrified of offending a stern God that you became scrupulous to the point of scrutinizing every one of your thoughts. And now place yourself in a community of adults that communicates to you in a thousand and one ways that the God of Jansenism is alive and well, and that your vocation in life is to make reparations to a God of justice. Is it any wonder that Pauline said the following about Thérèse's years in Carmel: "The fear of offending God was poisoning her life. Twice in her life, she confided to me that she was extremely happy. The first time was when she was about fifteen and a half, and Fr. Pichon, S.J., assured her that she had never committed a mortal sin. The second was at the 1891 retreat, when Fr. Alexis, a Recollect, taught her that her imperfections, which were all due to frailty, gave no offense to God."[114]

The context in which both Father Pichon and Father Alexis spoke to Thérèse was in the confessional. This is a significant fact because it indicates that Thérèse's problem with scruples was more episodic than continuous, and that her scruples were triggered by reflection upon her sinfulness that immediately preceded confession. Recall Marie's words, "It was especially on the eve of her confessions that they [Thérèse's scruples] recurred." It is also worth noting that the confession in which Father Pichon said to Thérèse "*In the presence of God, the Blessed Virgin, and all the Saints, I DECLARE THAT YOU HAVE NEVER COMMITTED A MORTAL SIN*" (S 149) was a general confession.

A general confession involves reviewing the whole of one's life, an exercise that scrupulous people should avoid. Furthermore, Thérèse went to confession to Father Alexis Prou during the community retreat of 1891, at which time she was tortured by doubts. "At the time I was having great interior trials of all kinds, even to the point of asking myself whether heaven really existed" (S 173). In other words, many of Thérèse's bouts with scruples were triggered during times of concentrated introspection and self-examination, often during community retreats where she heard frightening conferences reminiscent of the ones that she had heard when she was twelve. "Trust in God had become her special characteristic," testified Pauline. "[But] scruples came to paralyze this impetus, and she was very troubled, too, during her first years in Carmel. This was partly because she had heard it said in some sermons that it was very easy to offend God and to stain one's purity of conscience. This was a real torment to her."[115]

Pauline's statement gives us insight into one of Thérèse's interior struggles. We know that confidence and trust in God's love was a cornerstone of Thérèse's spirituality, but this does not mean that she always *felt* trust in God's love. Thérèse was like all of us. No matter how deeply we may believe in a merciful God, this belief is sometimes shaken. Think of times when you have heard a frightening sermon preached on hell or you have been yelled at in the confessional for a sin that you are ashamed of or recall a time when you were filled with guilt or remorse. At such times, did not a merciful God *recede* into the background and a God of stern justice come to the *fore*? Our emotions distort the countenance of the merciful God. Or as Julian of Norwich put it, there is no wrath in God; it is our guilt that makes us *feel* that God is angry with us.

Thérèse, like all of us, needed to be reassured over and over again that God is merciful. For example, when Fr. Alexis told Thérèse that her faults did not cause God any pain, Thérèse tells us that his words launched her "full sail upon the waves of *confidence and love*. . . . My nature was such that fear made me recoil; with *love* not only did I advance, I actually *flew*" (S 174). This passage can convey the erroneous impression that from this moment forward Thérèse never again recoiled in the face of her scruples. But this was not the case.

In a letter dated January 20, 1893 (fourteen months after Thérèse had heard Father Alexis's consoling words), Father

Pichon wrote the following to Thérèse in response to her doubts about being in the state of grace:

> Dear Child of my soul, listen to what I am about to tell you in the name and on the part of our Lord: No, no, you have not committed any mortal sins. I swear it. No, we cannot sin gravely without knowing it. No, after absolution, we must not doubt about our state of grace. To your mother St. Teresa, who was praying one day for souls, who were deluding themselves, our Lord answered: "My daughter, no one is lost without knowing it perfectly." Banish, then, your worries. God wills it, and I command it. Take my word for it: Never, never, never, have you committed a mortal sin. (L 767)[116]

What triggered the bout of scruples that is alluded to in this passage is not known. Perhaps it was something that the retreat master (Father Déodat) had said in one of his conferences during the recent community retreat (November 1892). Or perhaps it was the increased time for reflection that Thérèse had during her private retreat, which she made just prior to the community retreat.

Another possibility for what triggered Thérèse's scruples was the confrontation that she had with Sister Martha on December 8, 1892. Thérèse noticed that Sister Martha had developed an excessive attachment to Mother Gonzague and felt that God was asking her to speak to Sister Martha about the situation. Thérèse tells us that even though her confrontation with Sister Martha bore fruit, her words were very difficult for Sister Martha to bear. "The trial seemed very bitter to my poor companion" (S 237). And indeed it was. "Having listened awhile to these and other hard words," testified Sister Martha, "which I found very painful, I had to admit that what she said was very true."[117] We do not know how Sister Martha reacted to Thérèse's hard words, but we can surmise from what we know of Sister Martha that her reaction was not a mature one.

Sister Martha had lost both parents at an early age and had been passed from orphanage to orphanage. In consequence, she was emotionally unbalanced. All of her relationships were intense and went from one extreme to another. She either clung to people or rejected them. Her moods were mercurial; she could love someone one moment and hate her the next. Everyone in the community feared being on Sister Martha's bad side. Her violent temper and sharp tongue were not easy to bear.

Sister Martha was attracted to Thérèse, but she was also jealous of her. One day, Sister Martha would serve Thérèse leftovers that no one else would eat, and the next day she would invite Thérèse to warm herself by the kitchen stove. It is not hard to imagine Sister Martha punishing Thérèse after Thérèse confronted her about her relationship with Mother Gonzague. Sister Martha often sulked and treated others coldly when she was hurt. She knew that Thérèse was scrupulous and deathly afraid of offending God. What better way could Sister Martha punish Thérèse than to act coldly and make Thérèse feel guilty about what she had said?

If this was the case, it is easy to see why Sister Martha's behavior could throw Thérèse into a tailspin. For when we feel guilty for deeply hurting someone, we begin to question our judgment and even our motives. "Did God really want me to speak to Sister Martha? Was I too impulsive? Was it my overzealousness that blinded my judgment? Was my motive pure? Was I trying to get back at her for feeding me leftovers?" And on and on and on. We do not know for sure what triggered Thérèse's various bouts with scruples; the above is all conjecture, but the evidence that we do have points to the conclusion that Thérèse was vulnerable to attacks of scrupulosity all her life.

Thérèse's scrupulosity may be compared to self-esteem in our own lives. When life is going well and we are receiving affirmation in our work, we are not plagued by self-doubt. But let some failure trip us up or someone criticize us about what we have invested our self-worth in and then we are thrown into self-doubt. The vulnerable spots in our psyches are like dormant viruses. When we are healthy, they are fended off by our body's immune system, but under severe stress or when we are run down, they are activated. Such was the case with Thérèse's scrupulosity. When life was proceeding as usual, her scruples were under control, but when certain environmental factors were present (e.g., a Jansenistic retreat, being made to feel guilty for an action committed), Thérèse was thrown into self-doubt about the state of her soul. Thérèse's spirituality was rooted in her *belief* in Merciful Love, but she didn't always *feel* that God was merciful. Let us now examine the *choices* that Thérèse made in the face of her scruples.

The Temptation of Scruples. In May of 1889, Marie Guérin visited Paris. Like her cousin Thérèse, she was very scrupulous. While she was there, she became so scrupulous upon seeing statues and paintings of nudes that she felt that she could not receive the Eucharist. Knowing that Thérèse was also scrupulous, Marie wrote to Thérèse, asking her advice. Thérèse responded: "You did well to write to me, and I understand *everything . . . everything, everything, everything!* . . . You haven't committed the *shadow of any evil;* I know what these kinds of temptations are so well that I can assure you of this without any fear, and, besides, Jesus tells me this in the depths of my heart. . . . We must despise all these temptations and pay no attention whatsoever to them" (L 567).

To understand what Thérèse was saying, we need to differentiate the *object* of the scruple from the *temptation* that the scruple engenders. The object of the scruple, which is extremely common among scrupulous people, is sex. Thérèse tells Marie that she knows what she is talking about from her own experience. In this regard, Thérèse may have had in mind the time that she was in Paris en route to Rome. There she prayed to Our Lady of Victories to

> keep far from me everything that could tarnish my purity . . . [for] I could easily meet with things capable of troubling me. I was still unacquainted with evil and so was apprehensive about making its discovery. I had not yet experienced that *to the pure all things are pure,* that the simple and upright soul sees evil in nothing since it resides only in impure hearts, not in inanimate objects [statues, etc.]. (S 123)

Thérèse may also have been thinking of her bout with scruples that began during her second Communion retreat. As was said earlier, we do not know the content of her scruples, but there are several indications that they revolved around sex. First, scrupulosity regarding sex was prevalent in her family. Second, the retreat conferences focused on sins of impurity. Third, Thérèse was entering puberty, which may have been the crucial catalyst that triggered her scruples. The hormonal, physical, emotional, and psychological changes that accompany puberty could have been a significant factor in triggering Thérèse's scruples because of the confusion that they engendered. Thus, Thérèse could be very empathetic with Marie regarding the *object* of her scruples.

But what is the *temptation* of scruples? It is to *give in* to the scruples, to act on them. Because I *feel* that I have sinned grievously, I will not receive Communion. Marie asks: "How do you expect me to receive Holy Communion tomorrow and Friday? I am obliged to abstain from it" (L 566).

What is at stake in not giving in to scruples is the healing of one's image of God. The more we placate a wrathful god in order to avoid *feeling* guilty, the more power that god has over our lives. If Marie had given in to her scruples by choosing not to receive Communion and thus appease the God of Jansenism, her scruples would have been strengthened. By giving in to her scruples, she would have relieved her anxiety. In consequence, an *anxiety-relief* cycle would have been established.

Thérèse's advice to Marie was to go to Communion *in spite of* her fears. Thérèse writes,

> I hear you saying to me: "Thérèse is saying this because she doesn't know . . . she doesn't know I really do it on purpose . . . it pleases me . . . and so I cannot receive Communion since I believe I would commit a sacrilege. . . ." Yes, your poor little Thérèse does know; I tell you that she understands it *all,* and she assures you that you can go without any fear to receive your only true Friend. . . . She, too, has passed through the *martyrdom* of scruples, but Jesus has given her the grace to receive Communion just the same, even when she believed that she had committed *great sins.* . . . And so I assure you that she knew this was the sole means of ridding herself of the devil, for when he sees that he is losing his time, he leaves you in peace! . . . What offends [Jesus] and what wounds his heart is the lack of confidence! . . . Dear little sister, *receive Communion often,* very often. . . . That is the *only remedy* if you want to be healed, and Jesus hasn't placed this attraction in your soul for nothing. (L 568–69)

The *only remedy* of overcoming scruples can be interpreted in two ways. Literally, it refers to receiving the Eucharist. But pertaining to the *choice* that Marie must make in receiving the

Eucharist, it refers to not giving in to her fears. Here, Thérèse is alluding to a fundamental truth about the nature of fear. Namely, that the more we give in to our fears, the stronger they become. Conversely, the more that we choose to do God's will *in the face of fear,* the less hold fear has upon us. This truth applies to fear in general. But the specific fear that Thérèse is referring to is the fear of *feeling* guilty. I emphasize the word *feeling* because we can *feel* guilty without *being* guilty.

For example, we can *feel* guilty after we have confronted a person with a painful truth or given a just reprimand. At such times, we can be tempted to backpedal or soften the truth that we know God wanted us to speak. Thérèse recognized this temptation in her work with her novices:

> We should never allow kindness to degenerate into weakness. When we have scolded someone with just reason, we must leave the matter there, without allowing ourselves to be touched to the point of tormenting ourselves for having caused pain or at seeing one suffer and cry. To run after the afflicted one to console her does more harm than good. Leaving her to herself forces her to have recourse to God in order to see her faults and humble herself. Otherwise, accustomed to receiving consolation after a merited reprimand, she will always act, in the same circumstances, like a spoiled child, stamping her feet and crying until her mother comes to dry her tears. (LC 38–39)

Put yourself in Thérèse situation. You just made another person cry. How do you *feel*? What are you tempted to do? "Oh honey, I didn't mean what I said, please don't cry. That's okay. You go along and do what you feel you need to do." This is not an expression of compassion but of kindness that has degenerated into weakness. These words are not spoken for the sake of the person who feels hurt but for ourselves. We cannot bear *feeling* guilty.

We might not be scrupulous like Thérèse, but the underlying issue that she struggled with is our own—enduring feelings of false guilt as we choose to do God's will. For Thérèse, this was the only remedy. The same is true for us.

The Uncertain Certainty

"I DO NOT BELIEVE in eternal life," said Thérèse, "It seems to me that after this mortal life, there is nothing anymore." "Last evening, I was seized with a veritable anguish and my darkness increased. A voice said to me. 'Are you sure of being loved by God? Did he come and tell you?'"[118] She writes elsewhere:

> It seems to me that the darkness, borrowing the voice of sinners, says mockingly to me: "You are dreaming about the light, about a fatherland embalmed in the sweetest perfumes; you are dreaming about the *eternal* possession of the Creator of all these marvels; you believe that one day you will walk out of this fog that surrounds you! Advance, advance; rejoice in death which will give you not what you hope for but a night still more profound, the night of nothingness." (S 213)

"Frightful thoughts obsess me! . . . It's the reasoning of the worst materialists which is imposed upon my mind" (LC 257). "I want to do good after my death, but I will not be able to do so! It will be as it was for Mother Geneviève: We expected to see her work miracles, and complete silence fell over her tomb" (LC 257–58).

The above quotes are taken from the last eighteen months of Thérèse's life, a period in which she suffered agonizing doubts regarding the existence of heaven, the meaning of her vocation, and God's love for her. These doubts have commonly been referred to as Thérèse's "trial of faith." This is an unfortunate description, for it gives the impression that Thérèse's doubts were peculiar to this time in her life. This is not the case.

Thérèse experienced doubts about the existence of heaven all through religious life, and perhaps even prior to her entrance into Carmel.

Regarding her 1891 retreat, *five years* prior to her "trial of faith," Thérèse writes, "at the time I was having great interior trials of all kinds, even to the point of asking myself whether heaven really existed" (S 173). In the same vein, Thérèse tells us that the night before her profession of vows in 1890, "the darkness was so great that I could see and understand one thing only: I didn't have a vocation" (S 166). These two incidences of doubt may be regarded as illustrative of periods of doubt that are *not* recorded. In short, we should view Thérèse's trial of faith as an *intensification* and *prolongation* of what she had suffered many times throughout her life.

The first question that we will explore is what conditions *predisposed* Thérèse to having her trial of faith; what made her *susceptible?* The answer to this question can be summed up in one word, *stress*. At the onset of her trial of faith, Thérèse was exhausted as a result of physical, mental, and emotional stressors. Let us briefly explore these stressors in order to help us understand the context of Thérèse's trial of faith.

Major Stressors in Thérèse's Life at the Onset of her Trial of Faith. In the spring of 1894, Thérèse developed a persistent sore throat and a nagging cough, accompanied by frequent fevers that drained her physically (the first signs of her tuberculosis). During this time, Thérèse was also weighed down both mentally and emotionally. In May 1894, Thérèse's father suffered a heart attack. "This morning again," writes Céline, "Papa had an extremely violent attack while I was at Mass. . . . This attack was no longer a paralytic attack like the last one, it was a heart attack" (L 857). He died two months later. This was the culmination of what Thérèse referred to as "the *most bitter* and *most humiliating* of all chalices" (S 156), a chalice of suffering that had lasted for years.

Louis Martin had become mentally unstable in 1889. This necessitated his confinement to a mental asylum in Caen. Vicious rumors circulated that his mind had been eaten away by syphilis as a consequence of his sinful lifestyle. There was also gossip that he had become mentally unhinged when Thérèse entered Carmel. Thérèse was aware of these rumors for they were indiscreetly spoken of in her presence. Louis Martin, who had once been revered in Lisieux Carmel, became a source of embarrassment. "Silence settled more and more around the venerated name of him whom we loved," wrote Pauline. "In the Community where, until then, it had enjoyed a kind of prestige, if we pronounced it, it was in a whisper as though it were the name of a man almost in disgrace" (L 701).

In the two years that followed Louis's death in 1894, Thérèse's tuberculosis advanced. In April 1896, she had her first hemoptysis (spitting up blood). Around this time, Thérèse was burdened with three stressful events. The first was the election of the prioress. The community was so divided that the election dragged on for seven ballots. The two candidates were Mother Agnes (Pauline) and Mother Gonzague. Mother Gonzague won narrowly. But because she had *expected* to win easily, she felt betrayed by her community and considered leaving Lisieux for another Carmel. The election and its aftermath created an incredible amount of tension in the community, tension that Thérèse absorbed as she tried to minister to Mother Gonzague's wounded ego (see Thérèse's letter to Mother Gonzague dated June 20, 1896, L 958–62, "*Legend of a very little Lamb*"). This letter is a testimony to both Thérèse's compassion and her genius in dealing with a difficult situation. But as we all know, dealing with a person who feels betrayed and hurt is very taxing.

The letter also reveals Thérèse's great strength of character. Thérèse's sister Céline was due to make her profession just prior to the election, in which case her vows would have been accepted at the hands of Mother Agnes, the current prioress. But Mother Gonzague (Céline's novice mistress), feeling assured of victory, tried to postpone Céline's profession until after the election so that she could receive her vows. Thérèse was deeply incensed by what Mother Gonzague was trying to do. Sister Aimée remarked, "[Thérèse's] serenity was imperturbable. Only once did I see [her] lose this calm just a little. [When I said to Thérèse that] Mother Marie de Gonzague has a right to test Sister Geneviève (Céline), so why be surprised? Thérèse retorted with some feeling: 'There are some ways in which people should not be tested, and this is one of them.'"[119] How difficult it is to be kind and understanding to a person who has hurt someone we deeply love! This was the case with Thérèse in regard to Mother Gonzague.

The second stressor that was laid upon Thérèse's exhausted shoulders just prior to her first hemoptysis was being appointed novice mistress under Mother Gonzague, the newly elected prioress. Thérèse was now responsible for the formation of five novices, four of whom were her seniors. Thérèse felt overwhelmed. "When I was given the office of entering into the sanctuary of souls, I saw immediately that the task was beyond my strength" (S 237–38). And even though Thérèse found the strength that she needed in God, this did not alleviate the burdens that her office entailed. In this regard, one novice in particular should be mentioned—Sister Marie of the Trinity. Marie was a young Parisian who did not adjust easily to the demands of community life. She was fickle, superficial, highly emotional, and cried very easily. In short, she was a person who exacted much patience from Thérèse.

Finally, the third major stressor that Thérèse began to bear just prior to her first hemoptysis was working with Sister Marie of St. Joseph in the linen closet.

In Tolkien's *The Lord of the Rings,* Gandalf and his companions are exhausted from fighting orcs and trolls as they make their way through the treacherous mines of Moria when they are confronted with a Balrog, one of the most powerful forces of evil that lurks in the darkness. Gandalf leans wearily on his staff as he faces his foe. "'A Balrog,' muttered Gandalf. He faltered and leaned heavily on his staff. 'What an evil fortune! And I am already weary . . .' [In comparison to the Balrog, Gandalf] seemed small, and altogether alone: grey and bent, like a wizened tree before the onset of a storm."[120] Such was Thérèse when she began to fight her darkest foe; she was already exhausted from having fought many battles when her trial of faith began.

When we are sick, in low spirits, or emotionally distraught, our old fears, sorrows, self-doubts, antisocial behaviors and primitive appetites come to the fore. Under severe stress we regress. Thoughts, feelings, repressed memories, and psychological processes lay siege to our conscious mind, which under normal circumstances we have the strength to fend off and keep at bay. Thérèse's physical and emotional exhaustion was the condition that made her vulnerable to her trial of faith because it made her susceptible to her obsessive doubting. It was Thérèse's obsessive doubting, a part of her scrupulosity, that makes understandable the *sudden onset* of her trial of faith.

Thérèse was overjoyed when she awakened on Good Friday morning 1896 and discovered that she had spit up blood during the night. "Ah! my soul was filled with a great consolation. . . . the hope of going to heaven soon transported me with joy. . . . At this time I was enjoying such a living faith, such a clear *faith,* that the thought of heaven made up all my happiness, and I was unable to believe there were really impious people who had no faith. I believed they were actually speaking against their own inner convictions when they denied the existence of heaven" (S 211). But within *two days,* Thérèse's clear faith turned to utter darkness, and the thought of heaven that made up all of her happiness was now a "cause of struggle and torment" (S 211).

Thérèse's *conscious certitude* in the existence of heaven triggered an *unconscious doubt.* "But are you sure?" This doubt opened the floodgates of her unconscious. The mocking voice "borrowing the voice of sinners," and the "frightening thoughts . . . and reasonings of the worst materialists" that obsessed Thérèse did not come from *without* but from *within.* The frightening thoughts and feelings that Thérèse experienced during her trial of faith were not alien to her; rather, they were parts of her unconscious coming to consciousness. In order to understand Thérèse's doubts of faith from a psychological perspective, let us look at them through the lenses of two concepts taken from the school of Analytical (Jungian) psychology, namely, the *persona* and the *shadow.*

Persona and Shadow. In *War and Peace,* Tolstoy describes the experience of a teenage girl named Natasha attending the opera for the first time. At first, she is untainted by society's pretense and is able to see the unvarnished truth of what is set before her eyes. But by the end of the performance, all has changed.

> [At first], Natasha felt it all grotesque. . . . She could not follow the opera; she could not even listen to the music: she saw nothing but painted cardboard and strangely dressed-up

men and women, talking, singing, and moving about strangely. She knew what it all was meant to represent; but it was all so grotesquely false and unnatural that she felt ashamed and amused by the actors. She looked about her at the faces of the spectators, seeking in them signs of the same irony and bewilderment she was feeling in herself. But all the faces . . . expressed nothing but an affected, so Natasha thought, rapture. She looked at Ellen who sat gazing intently, with a quiet and serene smile. [Then] Natasha lost all sense of what she was and where she was and what was going on before her eyes. [At the end of the performance] every one clapped their hands and roared "bravo!" Then [Duport, the leading singer] stood alone [upon the stage]. Every one in the boxes and in the stalls began clapping and shouting with all their might, and Duport began smiling and bowing in all directions. Again a fearful uproar of applause arose among the spectators, and all began screaming with rapturous faces: "Duport! Duport! Duport!" Natasha no longer thought this strange. She looked about her with pleasure, smiling joyfully. "Isn't Duport admirable?" said Ellen, turning to her. "Oh yes," said Natasha.[121]

The metamorphosis that Natasha underwent, from being an innocent child, uncorrupted by affectation, who was able to see that the emperor had no clothes, to a sophisticated debutante who no longer knew what she really felt, is a symbol of what happens to all of us in the process of socialization. As we are impacted by the world around us, "the capacity to see and feel what is there," writes psychiatrist Ernest Schachtel, "gives way to the tendency to see and feel what one *is expected* to see and feel because everyone else does. Experience becomes predigested even before it is tasted."[122]

The town's people in Andersen's story, *The Emperor's New Clothes,* all pretend to see the nonexistent clothes of the emperor because they are told that anyone who is unable to see them is either "unfit for his office or unforgivably stupid."[123] The fear of being thought of as either incompetent or stupid created a pretense of silence. Because of fear, everyone denied the truth of his own eyes. The fear of what others will think of us is insidious. When we first don a mask, we are aware of our pretense. But over time, our awareness of our true thoughts and feelings is repressed.

As we grow up, it is communicated to us by our parents, authority figures, and our culture that certain beliefs, behaviors, ideas, expressions of affect, goals, and ideals are worthy of imitation. In consequence of our need to be accepted and our fear of being rejected, we incorporate into ourselves what is *expected* of us and *repress* what comes in conflict with these expectations. Jung terms the standards, mores, and goals of society that we have consciously identified with as the persona. Anything that is repressed in the unconscious because it comes in conflict with the persona is called the shadow. Robert Bly images the shadow as "the long bag we drag behind us."

> Let's talk about the personal shadow first. When we were one or two years old we had what we might visualize as a 360-degree personality. Energy radiated out from all parts of our body and all parts of our psyche. . . . but one day we noticed that our parents didn't like certain parts of that ball. They said things like: "Can't you keep still?" Or "It isn't nice to try to kill your brother." Behind us we have an invisible bag, and the part of us our parents don't like, we, to keep our parents' love, put in the bag. By the time we go to school our bag is quite large. Then our teachers

have their say: "Good children don't get angry over such little things." So we take our anger and put it in our bag. By the time my brother and I were twelve in Madison, Minnesota, we were known as "the nice Bly boys." Our bags were already a mile long. Then we do a lot of bag stuffing in high school. This time it's no longer the evil grownups that pressure us, but the people our own age. I lied all through high school automatically to try to be more like the basketball players. Any part of myself that was a little slow went into the bag. . . . So I maintain that out of the round globe of energy the twenty-year-old ends up with a slice. . . . We spend our life until twenty deciding what parts of ourself to put into the bag, and we spend the rest of our lives trying to get them out again. Suppose the bag remains sealed, what happens then? . . . When we put a part of ourselves in the bag it regresses. It de-evolves [and] regresses.[124]

In short, the shadow contains both the *repressed* and *underdeveloped* parts of our personality that have been discarded or neglected because they come in conflict with our persona; it contains all our impulses, desires, and character traits that our conscious personality disavows. The shadow is our *alter ego* and is commonly called "our double" because, as it gathers energy in the unconscious, it takes on a life of its own and functions as a separate personality. This may have been how Thérèse experienced her doubts. For does she not *personify* them as a "mocking voice?"

I know that this interpretation may sound strange to many of you, my dear readers, and some of you may even have an adverse reaction to it, as if I'm insinuating that Thérèse was mentally deranged because she was "hearing voices." I can assure you that the opposite is the case. I have encountered few people among the saints who are saner than Thérèse.

There is nothing necessarily abnormal about "hearing voices." As Carl Jung wrote, when repressed thoughts *emerge* to consciousness, they often "become audible as voices."[125] In various ways we all hear our shadow "speak." "I was so beside myself." "That was so out of character for me to say." "I just don't know what got into me today." "It just came out of me." These are all experiences of (and denials of) one's shadow. Would it not be more accurate to say, "What I just said was not *out* of character for me; rather, it *came out* of my character, that *part* of my character that I do not wish to acknowledge?" "No, nothing got *into* me today; rather, something came *out* of me." Similarly, Thérèse's doubts of faith came *out* of her. They were a part of her shadow surfacing to consciousness. Let us explore why Thérèse's doubts of faith were a part of her shadow. In order to do this, we must understand the age in which Thérèse lived.

The Age of Skepticism. From the time of the French Revolution in 1789, France became a country split into two groups: an anti-monarchical, anticlerical, liberal faction and the Catholic, monarchist, anti-republican faction. The Revolutionary government became increasingly hostile to the Church because the Church had allied itself to the monarchy. Consequently, the government sought to destroy the Church. The Church was exorcised from every social institution. The clergy were expelled from hospitals, schools, and other institutions. The Jesuits were suppressed; their twenty-eight colleges were closed, and military chaplaincies were abolished.

These attacks on the Church came to a head in Thérèse's lifetime. From 1879 to 1889, most religious congregations were dissolved, and religion was banned from public education. During the election of 1887, which gave rise to the Third Republic, the republican leader Léon Gambetta won the election on the campaign slogan, "Clericalism is the enemy!" Philosophical skepticism, deism, agnosticism, atheism, the widespread belief in the irrelevancy of the Christian creed, and the smoldering animosity of the populace toward the institutional church all chimed in and formed the "mocking voice" of Voltaire that was directed toward the Church. All of these factors worked together in secularizing the consciousness of France. Catholics quickly found themselves becoming a cognitive minority.

Three years after Thérèse's death, Paris inaugurated the new century by hosting the Universal Exposition that proclaimed a bold vision of global prosperity. Its blind optimism was fueled by breakthroughs in the various realms of science and technology that were wedded to a Darwinian vision of evolution and progress. For humanity to make progress, belief in the vision of modern science had to replace the abstract speculations of the philosophers and the outworn creed of Catholicism. Auguste Comte (1798–1857), who spearheaded positivistic philosophy in France, proposed a "Religion of Humanity" that would use the religious aspirations of the human heart to fuel the grand venture of scientific salvation.

Behind this emerging worldview lurked the question of the relevancy of God and religion that plagued Thérèse during her trial of faith. "[Science is] unceasingly making new advances, science will explain everything naturally; we shall have the absolute reason for everything that exists and that still remains a problem" (LC 257). If the thirteenth century can be labeled the age of belief, the nineteenth can be called the age of skepticism, and the French "made a specialty of skepticism," writes Will Durant.[126] But the spirit of the age was more than skeptical regarding the claims of religion; it regarded them as not worthy of consideration. Physics had replaced metaphysics as the realm of truth. That which could not be observed or measured was not worthy of inquiry. But the bright persona of this "new religion" had a dark shadow.

Nietzsche, who proclaimed that "God is dead," that is, belief in the existence of God is no longer tenable, recognized the shadow side of atheism that lurked behind its optimistic facade. If God is dead, then man is no longer shackled to a "slave morality" and is free to create a brave new world bereft of belief in a universal moral law. This made the world vulnerable to anarchy and nihilism. As Nietzsche wrote, "Morality was the greatest antidote against practical and theoretical nihilism."[127]

The shadow side of Nietzsche's proclamation of the "superman" was his prophecy of nihilism. Nietzsche's own philosophy drove him to despair because, as Ladislaus Boros put it, he had the *mind* of an atheist but the *heart* of a Christian.[128] He *believed* that God was dead and that man was accordingly free to shape his destiny unimpaired; however, living in a universe bereft of God made him *feel* abandoned and alone, overwhelmed by the absurdity of existence. Nietzsche, whom Thérèse called her "sick little brother," is a symbol of the psyche of nineteenth-century atheism. Its persona was optimism; its shadow was despair. The shadow side of the atheist's bold proclamation of *independence* from God was a cosmic form of *separation anxiety*. Belief in the supremacy of reason and the tools of science engendered in nineteenth-century man a dazzling dream of unending progress devoid of Christianity's vision of an Eternal Goal. Man had set a new course for himself but questioned where it would lead. Did it have a lasting purpose? Was there a "heaven?"

These were the questions of the age in which Thérèse lived and which haunted her mind.

But she also grew up in an embattled Church with a siege mentality, whose identity was formed in *opposition* to the forces seeking its demise. To be a good, loyal, strong Catholic in nineteenth-century France meant that one was not infected by the propaganda of the enemy—*doubts of faith*. Having doubts of faith was considered a threat to being a Catholic. Consequently, these doubts were denied and pushed out of consciousness as much as possible, which in turn formed part of the collective shadow of the Church. But repression is not absolute; it is relative. The wall that separates the conscious from the unconscious mind is not soundproof. It is like the wall that separates a child's bedroom from that of his parents. It admits snatches of conversations and tones of voice, which are not completely understood but nevertheless may arouse anxiety. This was the case with Thérèse.

Even though the walls of Les Buissonnets sequestered Thérèse from the outside world, they were not impermeable. Thérèse was very aware of the questions of her day. She must have often overheard discussions about church-state controversies between her father and her fiery uncle Isidore, who was very vocal in these matters and who devoted much of his time to writing editorials about them. In addition, Thérèse was taken up with the two prominent subjects of her age—history and science. "I applied myself to some special studies in *history* and *science,* and I did this on my own. The other studies left me indifferent, but these two subjects attracted all my attention; in a few months I acquired more knowledge than during my years of study" (S 101). Also, Thérèse was a precociously intelligent and reflective child who spent long periods of time thinking about the ultimate questions of existence. "*I thought.* . . . I think about God, about life, about ETERNITY . . . I *think*" (S 74).

Thérèse thought about what her contemporaries were saying about the afterlife and wondered if what they said was true. She *believed* in the promise of eternal life, but she had her *doubts*. "At the time I was having great interior trials of all kinds, even to the point of asking myself whether heaven really existed" (S 173). Thérèse shared with her contemporaries the doubts and anxieties about life having a lasting purpose. We can never know the exact character of Thérèse's great interior trials regarding her doubts about the existence of heaven for we do not have access to what she really experienced. Nevertheless, we can surmise that it brought her to the brink of despair because of what heaven symbolized for her.

First, heaven was the goal that oriented Thérèse's entire life; the promise of eternal life was the vision that gave purpose and meaning to her existence and sustained her in her sufferings. "It's upon heaven that everything bears" (LC 72), and without the promise of eternal life, existence was meaningless. During her trial of faith, Thérèse would have been able to understand Albert Camus's statement that: "There is but one truly serious philosophical problem, and that is suicide. Judging whether life is or is not worth living amounts to answering the fundamental question of philosophy."[129] "What a grace it is to have faith," says Thérèse. "If I had not had any faith, I would have committed suicide without an instant's hesitation" (LC 196).

Second, the prospect of heaven held out the hope to Thérèse that she would be reunited with her family and thus the deep wound of separation that had plagued her all of her life would be healed. Thérèse frequently spoke of earth as a place of exile and heaven as her homeland where she would be "reunited for all eternity in the heavenly Fatherland" (S 16). Heaven was the "*paternal home . . .* toward which the sighs of our hearts rise" (S 160).

Just as the deepest *desires* of our hearts have their corresponding *fears*, so too the object of our deepest *hope* is the potential object of our *despair*. Thus, if "the thought of heaven made up *all* of [Thérèse's] happiness," the prospect that heaven did not exist made up *all* of her sorrow (S 211, emphasis added). We can now understand why the thought that *maybe* heaven did not exist was so horrifying for Thérèse. Not only was such a doubt taboo in the Catholic culture in which Thérèse was reared, but it also corresponded to her deepest fear and thus had to be repressed as much as possible.

In summary, three factors worked together to produce Thérèse's trial of faith. First, her doubts in the existence of heaven gathered strength in her unconscious because they had been repressed. Second, Thérèse's physical and emotional exhaustion had so weakened her that her repressed doubts broke through to consciousness. Third, she could not dismiss her doubts because of her tendency toward obsessive doubting. During her trial of scruples, Thérèse tells us that, "as soon as I laid down my burden, I experienced peace for an instant; but this peace passed away like a lightening flash, and soon my martyrdom began over again" (S 84–85). This same dynamic took place in regard to her doubts of faith. "It is true that at times a very small ray of the sun comes to illumine my darkness, and then the trial ceases for *an instant,* but afterward the memory of this ray, instead of causing me joy, makes my darkness even more dense" (S 214). One of the places where Thérèse experienced these rays of light that relieved her darkness was in her dreams.

Dreams During Her Trial of Faith. One of the functions of dreams is compensation. That is, dreams help to offset, counteract, and rectify any imbalance that exists in our conscious life, be it our attitudes, perceptions, or beliefs. For example, if we have an inflated estimation of ourselves, our dreams will attempt to deflate our ego by portraying us in some inferior position. Conversely, if we underestimate our worth and gifts, our dreams will help to bolster our self-esteem in some symbolic way. Dreams are an expression of "the self-regulation of the psyche."[130] In short, there exists in our psyches a tendency that works to establish equilibrium, comparable to the one that exists in our bodies. If we look at the dreams that Thérèse had during her trial of faith, we can discern the compensatory function of dreams at work.

Thérèse's doubts about the existence of heaven filled her with anxiety because heaven symbolized the possibility of being reunited with loved ones (especially her mother and mother figures). Therefore, we would expect that the dreams that Thérèse had during her trial of faith would contain images of mother figures. This is precisely what we find.

Thérèse tells us that in her dreams during her trial of faith it was often the figure of Pauline (Thérèse's second mother) that comforted her. "I had a lot of nightmares last night, very frightful ones, but at the worst moment, you came to me and then I wasn't afraid" (LC 131). "I fell asleep and I dreamed you were bending over me to kiss me; I wanted to return the kiss, but all of a sudden I came awake" (LC 134). In another dream, Thérèse asks Pauline: "'And now I feel a cough threatening to come on! Finally! . . .' 'Everything is for the worst, isn't it?' [Pauline answered] . . . 'No, for the best.'" (LC 167). We also see various mother figures in Thérèse's dream of Venerable Ann of Jesus:

> At the first glimmerings of dawn I was (in a dream) in a kind of gallery and there were several other persons, but they were at a distance. Our mother was alone near me. Suddenly, without seeing how they had entered, I saw three Carmelites

dressed in their mantles and long veils. It appeared to me they were coming for our mother, but what I did understand clearly was that they came from heaven. In the depths of my heart I cried out: "Oh! how happy I would be if I could see the face of one of these Carmelites!" Then, as though my prayer were heard by her, the tallest of the saints advanced toward me; immediately I fell to my knees. Oh! what happiness! the Carmelite *raised her veil or rather she raised it and covered me with it.* Without the least hesitation, I recognized *Venerable Ann of Jesus,* Foundress of Carmel in France. Her face was beautiful but with an immaterial beauty. No ray escaped from it and still, in spite of the veil which covered us both, I saw this heavenly face suffused with an unspeakably gentle light, a light it didn't receive from without but was produced from within.

I cannot express the joy of my soul since these things are experienced but cannot be put into words. Several months have passed since this sweet dream, and yet the memory it has left in my soul has lost nothing of its freshness and heavenly charms. I still see Venerable Mother's glance and smile which was FILLED with LOVE. I believe I can still feel the caresses she gave me at this time. (S 190–91)

There are several references to "mother" in this dream. First, Thérèse says that she is standing next to "our mother." It is unclear to whom she is referring. It could be Zélie, since Thérèse is relating this dream to her blood sister Marie. Or it could possibly refer to Mother Gonzague, the current prioress. In either case, it refers to a significant mother-figure in Thérèse's life. Second, the prominent figure in the dream is the mother foundress of the Carmel in France, Venerable Ann of Jesus. Third, Venerable Ann's face is described in language similar to that which Thérèse had used to describe the face of the Blessed Mother as she had appeared to Thérèse during her cure at the age of ten. Thérèse not only emphasizes the celestial beauty of both faces but in particular mentions their smile. "The Blessed Virgin had appeared *very beautiful,* and I had seen her *smile at me*" (S 67). "I still see Venerable Mother's glance and smile which was FILLED with LOVE" (S 191). Finally, there is only one other time in Thérèse's life where she was covered with a veil as she was in the dream. Recall Pauline's clothing ceremony, when Thérèse "was able to contemplate [Pauline, her second mother] . . . under the white adornment of a Bride" (S 62).

When Thérèse awoke, the oppressive darkness had dissipated. The dark veil that stood between heaven and earth was rent, and Thérèse was filled with joy. "The storm was no longer raging. . . . I *believed,* I *felt* there was a *heaven* and that this *heaven* is peopled with souls who actually love me, who consider me their child" (S 191). Because she no longer felt *separated* from loved ones, especially her mother, Thérèse's darkness and anxiety subsided.

Spiritual Perspective. If we look at the last eighteen months of Thérèse's life through the Gospel criteria, "by their fruits you will know them," then it was the best of times for Thérèse spiritually, even though it was the worst of times for her physically, psychologically, and emotionally. For it was during this time, when Thérèse's body was being racked by tuberculosis and her mind was submerged in the darkness of doubt, that her spirit expanded under the impact of grace.

It is a far different reality to *believe* that "everything is a grace" (LC 57) than to *know* it by experience. During her trial of faith, Thérèse came to *know* that everything is a grace from God, even the grace to believe. Immediately prior to the onset of her trial of faith, the possibility that anyone could *not* believe in heaven was beyond Thérèse's comprehension. "I was unable to believe there were really impious people who had no faith. I believed they were actually speaking against their own inner convictions when they denied the existence of heaven" (S 211).

But as a result of her trial of faith, Thérèse came to call agnostics and atheists her brothers.

> Your child, however, O Lord, has understood Your divine light, and she begs pardon for her brothers. She is resigned to eat the bread of sorrow as long as You desire it; she does not wish to rise up from this table filled with bitterness at which poor sinners are eating until the day set by You. Can she not say in her name and in the name of her brothers, "*Have pity on us, O Lord, for we are poor sinners!*" (S 212)

The phrase "poor sinners" was used by French Catholics of Thérèse's day to refer to agnostics and atheists.

Clearly, Thérèse knew what it felt like to live in a universe that is a dead-end street, a road that leads to nowhere, a universe in which the grave is where it all ends. From what we have said thus far, we may conclude that during her night of faith, Thérèse participated in the skepticism of her age with all of its attending anguish and dread.

So what? Experiencing the darkness and anguish of others does not necessarily have any positive effects upon us. It can simply make us anxious and depressed. It was the *choices* that Thérèse made in the face of her darkness that made her trial of faith *redemptive*; it was how she *related to* her darkness that made it a *participation* in the paschal mystery. Thérèse did not simply *endure* the darkness; she chose to *embrace* it. Hers was no mere stoical abdication to fate but an acceptance of the cross. "She is resigned to eat the bread of sorrow as long as You desire it; she does not wish to rise up from this table filled with bitterness at which poor sinners are eating until the day set by You" (S 212).

Acts of faith are expressed in two ways. The first is our willingness *to jump into the darkness*, that is, choosing to trust in God's guidance as we venture into the unknown. The second is our willingness *to sit in the darkness*, which is continuing to do God's will when our emotional resources are depleted and life seems hollow, meaningless, and absurd. Thérèse was willing to sit in this darkness as long as God willed.

These are the worst of times in our life of faith when viewed from a psychological and emotional perspective. But from a spiritual vantage point, they have the potential to be the best of times. For when we continue to do God's will without emotional support, our love for God and neighbor grows and is purified. Thérèse expressed this truth in her poem *A Gloss on the Divine*, which she composed during her night of faith.

> Without support yet with support,
> Living without Light, in darkness,
> I am wholly being consumed by Love . . .
> I have no other Support than my God.
> And now I proclaim:
> What I value near Him
> Is to see and feel my soul
> Supported without any support![131]

In this poem, Thérèse touches upon one of the paradoxes of the spiritual life. It is at the point at which we are devoid of all human support and continue to say yes to God that we experience a support that is beyond the human. It is in those times of our lives when we do not have a drop of energy left to love our neighbor that, if we say *yes* to God, a divine energy wells up from within us.

Charity, which is the very life of God, came to perfection in Thérèse during her night of faith. Without the support of affect and the natural props that buoyed up her resolve and response to daily life, Thérèse chose to love her neighbor with what she called "*unfelt* love" (L 467), which is love that issues forth from the will alone. Recall that it was during her last year of life, while her body was being consumed by tuberculosis and her soul was shrouded in darkness, that she *volunteered* to work with Sister Marie of St. Joseph in the linen room. At the lowest point in her life, Thérèse was given the strength to *freely love* the most difficult person in her community. As she wrote a month after she terminated working with Sister Marie of St. Joseph, "this year, dear Mother, God has given me the grace to understand what charity is; I understood it before . . . but in an imperfect way" (S 219).

Similarly, Thérèse's faith came to fruition at the point at which she felt she had lost it. As theologian Karl Rahner said of Thérèse: "Here is a person who died in the mortal temptation to empty unbelief, right down to the roots of her being, and who *in* that condition believed."[132] Thérèse's doubts of faith were not *antithetical* to her faith but the *context* in which her faith matured.

We all know the nagging doubts that surround the precepts of faith and the haunting questions that attend upon whether or not life holds any ultimate meaning. Is there something beyond the grave? Or is life a tale told by an idiot, full of sound and fury, signifying *nothing*? The claim of immortality is either the most important fact of our existence or the biggest swindle that has ever been perpetrated upon the human race. Whether we feel that the former or later is true often depends upon the seasons of our lives. When all is going well, it is easy to believe in the existence of a bright horizon beyond the grave. But during the somber seasons of life, during periods of stress and sickness, or when the grayness of daily life has deeply seeped into our souls—we wonder. And like Thérèse, our doubts are not obstacles to faith but one of the *contexts* that tests its mettle.

The Undramatic Drama

IN 1884, GERARD MANLEY HOPKINS was appointed professor of Greek and Latin at University College in Dublin. From then until his death in 1889, Hopkins experienced the darkest years of his life. One of the causes of his darkness was the nature of the work to which he was assigned. It consisted of correcting Latin and Greek entrance exams, a Herculean task of tediousness. The exams, which were given six times a year, consisted of several pages of drab translation. Hopkins corrected nearly two thousand exams a year.

In the midst of this trial, Hopkins discovered a model of holiness in the recently canonized Jesuit lay brother St. Alphonsus Rodriguez. Rodriguez's life of undramatic fidelity helped Hopkins find meaning in his own life. For forty-six years, Alphonsus was the porter of the Jesuit college on the island of Majorca, where in patient obedience he "watched the door." In the last year of his life, Hopkins wrote a poem in honor of this quiet valor.

> HONOUR is flashed off exploit, so we say;
> And those strokes once that gashed flesh or galled shield
> Should tongue that time now, trumpet now that field,
> And, on the fighter, forge his glorious day.
> On Christ they do and on the martyr may;
> But be the war within, the brand we wield
> Unseen, the heroic breast not outward-steeled,
> Earth hears no hurtle then from fiercest fray.
> Yet God (that hews mountain and continent,

Earth, all, out: who, with trickling increment,
Veins violets and tall trees makes more and more)
Could crowd career with conquest while there went
Those years and years by of world without event
That in Majorca Alfonso watched the door.[133]

Each of us fights a "war within," the cost of which no one knows but God alone. Not as man sees does God see, because man sees the appearance but the Lord looks into the heart (1 Sam 16:7). Judged by the standards of this world, our lives look like a "world without event," but to God alone is known the "the heroic breast." All of us can say with Thérèse, "Ah! what a surprise we shall have at the end of the world when we shall read the story of souls! There will be those who will be surprised when they see the way through which my soul was guided!" (S 149).

Our real life is that which is known to God alone and not that which is judged by the standards of this world. In Act IV of *King Lear,* there appears upon the stage a character who is so insignificant that Shakespeare doesn't even give him a name; he is simply referred to as the First Servant. As he witnesses Gloucester being blinded, the First Servant draws his sword to defend his master but is mortally stabbed in the back by Goneril. His whole part consists of only eight lines, none of which are quoteworthy.

No one remembers the First Servant. But if *King Lear* were not a play but *real life*, then his part would have been the best to have played. For it is not important that we are lauded or remembered by this passing world, for all that the world affords is fleeting. "The boast of heraldry, the pomp of power, / And all that beauty, all that wealth e'er gave, /Awaits alike the inevitable hour: / The paths of glory lead but to the grave."[134]

The only glory that survives the grave is a life well lived. In a hundred years it will not have made any difference how much money we have in the bank, how many cars we have in the garage, how much power we wielded in our jobs, how many books we have written, or how esteemed we were by colleagues and friends. The only thing that ultimately matters is whether or not we have done the will of God.

In this book, I have tried to show through the life of one woman that the trials and tragedies of life, the fears and conflicts of the human heart are not obstacles to growth in holiness but the stage upon which the drama of holiness unfolds. The same is true for us. The gray mundaneness of daily life, our wounded psyches with all their fears and neurotic conflicts, our families, friends, and peers who never live up to our expectations and who often disappoint us, the impersonal and insecure world that we live in, is the *context* in which we choose to do God's will.

"Drama's Vitallest Expression is the Common Day," writes Emily Dickinson.[135] And the common day is *the* expression of the drama of life because it is the *only* stage upon which the drama unfolds. But common does not mean insignificant or inconsequential, for "the trivialness of life is . . . done away by the Incarnation."[136]

This vital truth is proclaimed by the life of St. Thérèse. To all appearances, her life was uneventful. Even many of the nuns who lived with Thérèse did not recognize anything extraordinary about her. Shortly before she died, Thérèse overheard one nun say to another, "Sister Thérèse will die soon; what will our mother prioress be able to write in her obituary notice? She entered our convent, lived and died—there really is no more to say."[137] How ironically accurate is this summation of Thérèse's life. She *lived!*

Thérèse lived life to the fullest because she lived deliberately. "[I do not allow] one little sacrifice to escape, not one look, one word, profiting by all the smallest things and doing them through love" (S 196).

"As you have seen I came from a sheltered life. But a sheltered life can be a daring life as well. For all serious daring starts from within."[138] These concluding words of Eudora Welty's autobiography could very well have been the concluding words of *Story of a Soul*. For though Thérèse lived a sheltered life, it was a daring life. She dared to do the will of God in the midst of life's difficulties—*the context of holiness*.

Notes

1. Evelyn Underhill, *The Spiritual Life* (Wilton, Conn.: Morehouse Barlow Co., 1955), 11.
2. Abbé de Tourville, *Letters of Direction* (Wilton, Conn.: Morehouse Barlow Co., 1939), 51.
3. Josef Pieper, *Guide to St. Thomas,* trans. Richard and Clara Winston (San Francisco: Ignatius Press, 1986), 51.
4. St. John of the Cross, "The Ascent of Mount Carmel," in *The Collected Works of St. John of the Cross*, trans. Kieran Kavanaugh, O.C.D., and Otilio Rodriguez, O.C.D. (Washington, D.C.: ICS Publications, 1991), Prol. 2, 115.
5. Separation anxiety has appeared in infants as early as one month of age. Its onset depends upon both the maturation of the infant and the nature of the emotional bond that exists between mother and child.
6. Guy Gaucher, *The Story of a Life: St. Thérèse of Lisieux,* trans. Anne Marie Brennan (San Francisco: Harper & Row, 1987), 15.
7. "There is abundant evidence that after a child has been away from home in a strange place in the care of strangers he is liable to be very frightened lest he be taken away again." John Bowlby, *Attachment and Loss* (n.p.: Basic Books, 1980), 13.
8. It is also noteworthy that Thérèse selected these two passages from her mother's letters as a part of her self-portrait in *Story of a Soul* (S 23).
9. Sister Geneviève of the Holy Face (Céline Martin), *The Mother of the Little Flower*, trans. Michael Collins, S.M.A. (Dublin: M. H. Gill and Sons Ltd., 1957), 75.

10. Marie Baudouin-Croix, *Léonie Martin: A Difficult Life,* trans. Mary Frances Mooney (Dublin: Veritas Publications, 1993), 19.
11. Baudouin-Croix, 20.
12. Harry Stack Sullivan, *The Interpersonal Theory of Psychiatry* (New York: W. W. Norton and Company, 1953), 41.
13. Theodore Millon with Rogers D. Davis, *Disorders of Personality DSM-IV and Beyond* (New York: John Wiley & Sons, 1996), 266–67.
14. Sandra Cisneros, "Eleven," in *Woman Hollering Creek: And Other Stories* (New York: Vintage Books, 1991), 6–7.
15. Sister Geneviève of the Holy Face (Céline Martin), *The Father of the Little Flower,* trans. Michael Collins, S.M.A. (Dublin: M. H. Gill and Sons, 1955), 34.
16. Stephen A. Mitchell and Margaret J. Black, *Freud and Beyond: A History of Psychoanalytic Thought* (New York: Basic Books, 1995), 67–68.
17. T. S. Eliot, "Little Gidding," in *Four Quartets* (New York: Harcourt, Brace, Jovanovich, 1971), 54.
18. Baudouin-Croix, *Léonie Martin,* 91.
19. Charles Dickens, *A Christmas Carol and Other Christmas Stories* (New York: Penguin Books, 1984), 71.
20. William Wordsworth, "Lines Written a Few Miles above Tintern Abbey," in *William Wordsworth,* ed. Stephen Gill (Oxford: Oxford University Press, 1984), 132.
21. Alfred Adler, *Social Interest: A Challenge to Mankind,* trans. John Linton, M.A. and Richard Vaughan (New York: G. P. Putnam's Sons, 1964), 208.
22. William Wordsworth, "Ode," in *William Wordsworth,* ed. Stephen Gill (Oxford: Oxford University Press, 1984), 301.

23. Ida Friederike Görres, *The Hidden Face: A Study of St. Thérèse of Lisieux*, trans. Richard and Clara Winston (New York: Pantheon Books, 1959), 169. Jung held that the psyche is a self-regulating system in which the unconscious automatically tries to compensate or offset any imbalance in our conscious life. Jung writes: "The psyche is a self-regulating system that maintains its equilibrium just as the body does. Every process that goes too far immediately and inevitably calls forth compensations. . . . When we set out to interpret a dream, it is always helpful to ask: what conscious attitude does it compensate?" Carl Jung, *Dreams,* trans. R. F. C. Hall (Princeton: Princeton University Press, 1974), 101.
24. Perhaps one of the reasons why the story of *The Golden Trial* came to Thérèse's mind was because the protagonist of the story (a little girl named Marie) had a dream in which "a vivid picture of her mother came to her mind. She was alone, so abandoned, so miserable and the sad remembrance of a time when her sick mother could neither look after her nor care for her arose in her memory" (translated by Sister Mary of the Heart of Jesus and of the Holy Face, Pewaukee Carmel). Would not this passage bring to Thérèse's mind the memory of Zélie's sickness and death?
25. William James, *Principles of Psychology* (New York: Henry Hold & Company, 1908), 128.
26. James, 125.
27. Augustine Maurer, C.S.B., *About Beauty: A Thomistic Interpretation* (Houston: Center for Thomistic Studies, 1983), 116.
28. Gustave Flaubert, *Madame Bovary,* trans. Francis Steegmuller (New York: Quality Paperback Book Club, 1991), 40–41.
29. John Keats, "Ode on a Grecian Urn," in *John Keats and Percy Bysshe Shelley: Complete Poetical Works* (New York: Modern Library, 1967), 186.

30. Mortimer J. Adler, *Six Great Ideas* (New York: Macmillan Publishing Company, 1981), 130.
31. Timothy Ferris, *The Whole Shebang: A State-of-the-Universe(s) Report* (New York: Simon & Schuster, 1997), 27.
32. Richard Feynman, *The Character of Physical Law* (Cambridge, Mass.: MIT Press, 1965), 14.
33. William Wordsworth, "Ode," 302.
34. Harold S. Kushner, *When Bad Things Happen to Good People* (New York: Schocken Books, 1981), 69.
35. Dante Alighieri, *The Paradiso,* trans. John Ciardi (New York: The New American Library, 1970), canto 32, pp. 250–51. Mentally viewing events from a distance is a basic technique used by Neutro-Linguistic Programming to help decrease anxiety, anger, etc. See Richard Bandler, *Using Your Brain for a Change,* ed. Connirae Andreas and Steve Andreas (Moab, UT: Real People Press, 1985).
36. Charles Dickens, *Great Expectations* (New York: Bantam Books, 1981), 66.
37. Sister Geneviève of the Holy Face (Célene Martin), *A Memoir of My Sister St. Thérèse,* trans. Carmelite Sisters of New York (New York: P.J. Kennedy and Sons, 1959), 138.
38. Wallace Stevens, "Sunday Morning," in *The Collected Poems of Wallace Stevens* (New York: Alfred A. Knopf, 1969), 69.
39. Walter de la Mare, "Fare Well," in *Selected Poems* (London: Faber & Faber, 1954), 54.
40. "Most experts in child psychology recognise that play is related to the child's current capacities for satisfactory adjustment, as well as prognostic of future adjustment." *Personality Development and Psychopathology: A Dynamic Approach*, 2nd ed., ed. Norman Cameron and Joseph F. Rychlak (Boston: Houghton Mifflin Company, 1985), 83.

41. Christopher O'Mahony, ed. and trans., *St. Thérèse of Lisieux: By Those Who Knew Her* (Dublin: Veritas Publications, 1975), 111.
42. O'Mahony, 111.
43. O'Mahony, 114.
44. O'Mahony, 114.
45. René Spitz, "Anaclitic Depression: An Inquiry into the Genesis of Psychiatric Conditions in Early Childhood," in *Psychodynamic Understanding of Depression,* ed. Willard Gaylin (New York: Jason Aronson, 1983), 224.
46. Thérèse is quoting from St. John of the Cross's poem *Glosa a lo divino.* "After I have known it / love works so in me / that whether things go well or badly / love turns them to one sweetness transforming the soul into itself."
47. Alfred Adler, *The Education of Children,* trans. Rudolph Dreikurs, MD (South Bend: Gateway Editions, Ltd., 1930), 12.
48. O'Mahony, *St. Thérèse of Lisieux,* 51.
49. F. Scott Fitzgerald, *The Great Gatsby* (New York: Macmillan Publishing Company, 1925), 1.
50. O'Mahony, *St. Thérèse of Lisieux,* 51.
51. O'Mahony, 94.
52. O'Mahony, 51.
53. Pere Liagre, C.S.Sp., *A Retreat with St. Thérèse,* trans. Dom P. Owen, O.S.B. (Westminster, Md.: The Newman Bookshop, 1948), 43.
54. Teilhard de Chardin, *The Divine Milieu* (New York: Harper and Row, 1960), 56.
55. "My house is at rest" is a reference to a line from St. John of the Cross's poem *The Dark Night.*
56. O'Mahony, *St. Thérèse of Lisieux,* 131.
57. Peter Shaffer, *Amadeus* (New York: New American Library, 1981), Act 2, Scene 17, p. 147, & Act 1, Scene 12, p. 74.

58. Alfred Adler contended that a person's earliest memories are windows into understanding a person's characterological dispositions and interpretations about life. "Memories can never run counter to [a person's] style of life. . . . The first memory will show his fundamental view of life." *The Individual Psychology of Alfred Adler: A Systematic Presentation in Selections from His Writings,* ed. Heinz L. Ansbacher and Rowena R. Ansbacher (New York: Harper Torchbooks, 1956), 351. Adler also said that it is irrelevant whether or not the memories are real or fictional because our memories are chosen and configured to reflect our image of self, the world, and our stance toward life. Thus, if we look at Thérèse's early memory of her trip to Le Mans from the viewpoint of what it reveals about Thérèse's self-image, we see a child who views herself as one who is overwhelmed to the point of tears because no one can understand her grief. The self-image of a person who believes that her grief is so deep that she cannot be understood by mere mortals, gradually and unconsciously begins to fashion both her strategies for security and the basis of her significance.

59. Robert J. Giugliano, PhD, "Separation, Loss, and Longing in the Infancy and Early Childhood of St. Thérèse of the Child Jesus and the Holy Face: Attachment in Psychological and Spiritual Development," Master of Arts in Religion and Religious Education, Fordham University, 2004, p. 136.

60. In his clinical practice, Kohut noticed that his clients felt a sense of inner cohesion whenever he either showed them empathic admiration (*mirroring*) or allowed himself to be seen as an all-powerful, wise human being (*idealizing*). From these experiences, Kohut postulated that the psyche has a *bipolar self-structure,* that is, it has two fundamental needs by which we connect with other people. The first is *mirroring,* which in its archaic form is the need that the child's *grandiose self* has for constant attention and perfect admiration and the need

to feel that one is the center of the universe. When this need matures and is internalized, it becomes the basis of self-esteem and self-assertive ambitions; it is the memory that one is special. In healthy people, the need for mirroring will persist, for we all need encouragement and positive feedback, but for "mirror hungry" people, people who did not receive adequate mirroring when they were young, the need for mirroring will continue to exist in its archaic form.

The second need that Kohut postulated was what he called *idealizing needs*, which is rooted in the child's *idealized parental imago*. In its archaic form, the need to *idealize* is the need to merge with a calming, all-powerful idealized figure. As children, we all need to attach ourselves to "superheroes" in order to feel protected in a menacing world and to feel significant by virtue of being connected to a superior human being ("I must be wonderful if my friend is wonderful"). When this need matures, it internalizes itself in the form of our ideals.

Kohut postulated that the nuclear self is made up of the psyche's *grandiose self* at one pole, and the *idealized parental imago* at the other pole. Out of these two poles arise two basic needs: the need to be affirmed (*mirroring*), from which our ambition for success develops, and our need for idealized figures (*idealizing*), from which our ideals are formed. Kohut posited a *tension-arc* between the two poles, that is, between our ambitions and goals; it is the tension of living between the *real* and the *ideal*.

There are two consequences when our *mirroring* and *idealizing* needs are transmuted and internalized. First, we can maintain a healthy self-esteem without being the center of the universe. Second, our world will not fall apart when we discover that none of our heroes and heroines are gods and goddesses, but are good human beings with clay feet.

61. Charles Dickens, *Great Expectations* (New York: Bantam Books, 1981), ch. 27, 209.
62. Bruno Bettelheim, *The Uses of Enchantment: The Meaning and Importance of Fairy Tales* (New York: Alfred A. Knopf, 1977), 144.
63. Fritz Kunkel, *Selected Writings*, ed. John A. Sanford (New York: Paulist Press, 1984), 83 and 86.
64. F. Scott Fitzgerald, "The Long Way Out," in *The Stories of F. Scott Fitzgerald* (New York: Macmillan Publishing Company, 1951), 444 and 446.
65. Charles Dickens, "The Wreck of the Golden Mary," in *Christmas Stories by Charles Dickens* (Oxford: Oxford University Press, 1987), 154.
66. Carl Rogers, *A Way of Being* (Boston: Houghton Mifflin Company, 1980), 10.
67. O'Mahony, *St. Thérèse of Lisieux*, 172.
68. Görres, *The Hidden Face*, 419.
69. Josef Breuer and Sigmund Freud, *Studies in Hysteria*, in *The Standard Edition of the Complete Works of Sigmund Freud*, vol. 2, trans. James Strachey (London: The Hogarth Press and the Institute of Psychoanalysis, 1955), xxvi.
70. Erich Fromm, *Greatness and Limitations of Freud's Thought* (New York: New American Library, 1980), 24.
71. Alexander Lowen, MD, writes: "In the forty years I have worked as a therapist, I have seen a marked change in the personality problems of the people consulting me. The neuroses of earlier times, represented by incapacitating guilts, anxieties, phobias, or obsessions are not commonly seen today. Instead, I see more people who complain of depression; they describe a lack of feeling, an inner emptiness, a deep sense of frustration and unfulfillment." Lowen, *Narcissism: Denial of the True Self* (New York: Collier Books, 1983), x.

72. Breuer and Freud, *Studies in Hysteria*, 6, 10, emphasis added.
73. Gaucher, *The Story of a Life*, trans. Anne Marie Brennan (San Francisco: Harper & Row, 1987), 47.
74. Norman Cameron and Joseph F. Rychlak, *Personality Development and Psychopathology*, 2nd ed. (Boston: Houghton Mifflin Company, 1985), 522.
75. Breuer and Freud, *Studies in Hysteria*, 6.
76. T. S. Eliot, "Burnt Norton," in *Four Quartets* (New York: Harcourt, 1971), 14.
77. Peter L. Giovacchini, MD, *A Narrative Textbook of Psychoanalysis* (Northvale, N.J.: Jason Aronson, 1987), 221.
78. This is a finding of Aaron T. Beck's research on clinical depression.
79. William Wordsworth, "Ode," 302.
80. Breuer and Freud, *Studies in Hysteria*, 11.
81. Breuer and Freud, 9.
82. Breuer and Freud, 7.
83. Sigmund Freud, *Inhibitions, Symptoms, and Anxiety*, trans. Alex Strachey (New York: W. W. Norton & Company, 1959), 57.
84. Harold F. Searles, *My Work with Borderline Patients* (Northvale, N.J.: Jason Aronson, 1986), 8.
85. Breuer and Freud, *Studies in Hysteria*, 17.
86. St. Augustine, *The Essential Augustine*, ed. Vernon J. Bourke (New York: New American Library, 1964), 22.
87. O'Mahony, *St. Thérèse of Lisieux*, 173.
88. William Butler Yeats, "Meditations in Time of Civil War," in *The Collected Poems of W. B. Yeats* (New York: Macmillian Publishing Company, 1956), 198–99.
89. Louis had removed Thérèse from boarding school; he was afraid that Thérèse would suffer a relapse if she remained there. Besides the stress that Thérèse had undergone at

school, there were two additional factors that increased this stress and may have contributed to Louis's decision to remove her from the boarding school. First, Céline had graduated from the boarding school, and, therefore, was not able to provide Thérèse with the emotional support that her presence had afforded. Second, Thérèse was suffering from a severe case of scruples that had been generated by a retreat given at the school.

90. Charles Dickens, "Dullborough Town," in *The Uncommercial Traveller,* in *Selected Short Fiction,* ed. Deborah A. Thomas (New York: Penguin Books, 1985), 212.

91. The myth of Icarus can be found in Book VIII of Ovid's *Metamorphoses.*

92. W. H. Auden, "Musée Des Beaux Arts," in *Selected Poems,* ed. Edward Mendelson (New York: Vintage Books, 1976), 79.

93. William Carlos Williams, "Landscape with the Fall of Icarus," in *The Collected Poems of William Carlos Williams,* vol. 2, *1939-1962,* ed. Christopher MacGowan (New York: New Directions Books, 1988), 385–86.

94. Robert Bly, James Hillman, and Michael Meade, eds., *The Rag and Bone Shop of the Heart: Poems for Men* (New York: Harper Perennial, 1992), 475.

95. Görres, *The Hidden Face,* 107.

96. O'Mahony, *St. Thérèse of Lisieux,* 57.

97. Hans Christian Anderson, "The Princess and the Pea," in *The Complete Fairy Tales and Stories,* trans. Erik Christian Haugaard (Garden City, N.Y.: Anchor Press/Doubleday, 1983), 20.

98. Helen Luke, "Courtesy," in *Kaleidoscope: The Way of Women* (New York: Parabola Books, 1992), 190.

99. Dante, *Purgatory,* trans. Dorothy Sayers (Baltimore: Penguin Books, 1955), canto III, 88.

100. Obsessive doubting is a symptom of obsessive-compulsive disorder, of which scrupulosity is a species. For further reading on the relationship between scrupulosity and obsessive compulsive disorders, see Joseph W. Ciarrocchi, *The Doubting Disease: Help for Scrupulosity and Religious Compulsions* (New York: Paulist Press, 1995); and William Van Ornum, *A Thousand Frightening Fantasies: Understanding and Healing Scrupulosity and Obsessive Compulsive Disorder* (New York: Crossroad Publishing Company, 1997).
101. Conrad De Meester, O.C.D., ed., *Saint Thérèse of Lisieux: Her Life, Times, and Teaching* (Washington, D.C.: ICS Publications, 1997), 12.
102. De Meester, 13.
103. De Meester, 13.
104. Sister Geneviève, *The Mother of the Little Flower*, 1.
105. Joseph W. Ciarrocchi, *The Doubting Disease: Help for Scrupulosity and Religious Compulsions* (New York: Paulist Press, 1995), 27.
106. For a good analysis of this subject, see Conrad De Meester, O.C.D., *The Power of Confidence*, trans. Susan Conroy (New York: Alba House, 1998), esp. 361–65.
107. Sister Geneviève, *The Mother of the Little Flower*, 4.
108. James Joyce, *A Portrait of the Artist as a Young Man* (Mattituck, New York: The American Reprint Company, 1944), 119–23.
109. William Van Ornum, *A Thousand Frightening Fantasies: Understanding and Healing Scrupulosity and Obsessive Compulsive Disorder* (New York: Crossroad Publishing Company, 1997), 78.
110. O'Mahony, *St. Thérèse of Lisieux*, 88.
111. O'Mahony, *St. Thérèse of Lisieux*, 208, emphasis added.
112. William Wordsworth, "Lines Written a Few Miles above Tintern Abbey," 134.

113. Abbé André Combes, *St. Thérèse and Her Mission*, trans. Alastair Guinan (New York: P. J. Kennedy & Sons, 1955), 134–35.
114. O'Mahony, *St. Thérèse of Lisieux*, 44.
115. O'Mahony, 42–43.
116. Similarly, in a letter dated October 4, 1889 (sixteen months after Father Pichon told Thérèse that she had never committed a mortal sin), Father Pichon wrote to Thérèse the following: "I forbid you in the name of God to call into question your being in the state of grace. The devil is laughing heartily at you. I protest against this ugly mistrust. Believe obstinately that Jesus loves you" (L 585).
117. O'Mahony, *St. Thérèse of Lisieux*, 223.
118. Emmanuel Renault, O.C.D., "Thérèse in the Night of Faith," in *Saint Thérèse of Lisieux: Her Life, Times, and Teaching*, ed. Conrad De Meester, O.C.D. (Washington, D.C.: ICS Publications, 1997), 22, 78.
119. O'Mahony, 280.
120. J. R. R. Tolkien, "The Fellowship of the Rings," in *The Lord of the Rings* (New York: Ballantine Books, 1965), 428–29.
121. Leo Tolstoy, *War and Peace,* trans. Constance Garnett (New York: New Modern Library, 1962), part 8, ch. 9, 524–27.
122. Ernest G. Schachtel, "On Memory and Childhood Amnesia," in *An Outline of Psychoanalysis,* ed. Clara Thompson (New York: New Modern Library, 1955), 211, emphasis added.
123. Hans Christian Andersen, "The Emperor's New Clothes," in *Hans Christian Andersen: The Complete Fairy Tales and Stories*, trans. Erik Christian Haugaard (Garden City, N.Y.: Anchor Press/Doubleday, 1983), 77.
124. Robert Bly, *A Little Book on the Human Shadow* (San Francisco: Harper & Row, 1988), 17–19.

125. Carl Jung, "Two Essays in Analytical Psychology," in *The Collected Works of C. G. Jung,* vol. 7 (Princeton: Princeton University Press, 1966), 282. See also, "The Structure and Dynamics of the Psyche," in *The Collected Works of C. G. Jung,* vol. 8 (Princeton, N.J.: Princeton University Press, 1969), esp. 88–89: "Thus, in coming to terms with the unconscious, not only is the standpoint of the ego justified but the unconscious is granted the same authority. The ego takes the lead, but the unconscious must be allowed to have its say too—*audiatur et altera pars.* The way this can be done is best shown by those cases in which the 'other' voice is more or less distinctly heard" (88).

126. Will Durant, *The Story of Philosophy* (New York: Washington Square Press, 1961), 351.

127. Frederick Copleston, S.J., *A History of Philosophy,* vol. 7, *Modern Philosophy,* part 1, *Fichte to Hegel* (Garden City, N.Y.: Image Books, 1963), 180.

128. Ladislaus Boros, *Open Spirit,* trans. Erika Young (New York: Paulist Press, 1974), 62.

129. Albert Camus, *The Myth of Sisyphus and Other Essays,* trans. Justin O'Brien (New York: Vintage Books, 1955), 3.

130. Carl Jung, "General Aspects of Dream Psychology," in *The Collected Works of C. G. Jung,* vol. 8, 253.

131. Thérèse of Lisieux, *The Poetry of Saint Thérèse of Lisieux,* trans. Donald Kinney, O.C.D. (Washington, D.C.: ICS Publications, 1996), 148.

132. Patrick Ahern, *Maurice and Thérèse: The Story of a Love* (New York: Image Books, 1998), 101.

133. Gerard Manley Hopkins, "St. Alphonsus Rodriguez," in *Gerard Manley Hopkins: Poems and Prose,* ed. W. H. Gardner (Baltimore: Penguin Books, 1967), 66–67.

134. Thomas Gray, "Elegy written in a Country Churchyard," in *Elegy in a Country Churchyard and other writings,* (London: Orion Books, 1966), 7.
135. Emily Dickinson, Poem 741, "Drama's Vitallest Expression is the Common Day," in *The Complete Poems of Emily Dickinson* (Boston: Little Brown, 1960), 363.
136. *The Letters of Gerard Manley Hopkins to Robert Bridges,* ed. and intro. Claude C. Abbott (London: Oxford University Press, 1955), 19.
137. Görres, *The Hidden Face,* 1.
138. Eudora Welty, *One Writer's Beginnings* (Cambridge, Mass.: Harvard University Press, 1984), 104.

About Us

ICS Publications, based in Washington, D.C., is the publishing house of the Institute of Carmelite Studies (ICS) and a ministry of the Discalced Carmelite Friars of the Washington Province (U.S.A.). The Institute of Carmelite Studies promotes research and publication in the field of Carmelite spirituality, especially about Carmelite saints and related topics. Its members are friars of the Washington Province.

Discalced Carmelites are a worldwide Roman Catholic religious order comprised of friars, nuns, and laity—men and women who are heirs to the teaching and way of life of Teresa of Ávila and John of the Cross, dedicated to contemplation and to ministry in the church and the world.

Information about their way of life is available through local diocesan vocation offices, or from the Discalced Carmelite Friars vocation directors at the following addresses:

Washington Province:
1525 Carmel Road, Hubertus, WI 53033

California-Arizona Province:
P.O. Box 3420, San Jose, CA 95156

Oklahoma Province:
5151 Marylake Drive, Little Rock, AR 72206

Visit our websites at:

www.icspublications.org   and   *http://ocdfriarsvocation.org*

Notes

Notes